CRIMES IN THE NAME OF LIBERTY

THE DICTATORSHIP OF WESTERN DEMOCRACIES AND THE SUFFERING IT CAUSES AROUND THE WORLD

Pascal KONNEH

To order additional copies of this book, contact:
Xlibris
UK TFN: 0800 0148620 (Toll Free inside the UK)
UK Local: 02036 956328 (+44 20 3695 6328 from outside the UK)
www.Xlibrispublishing.co.uk
Orders@Xlibrispublishing.co.uk
755666

CRIMES IN THE NAME OF LIBERTY

O Liberté, que de crimes on commet en ton nom!
(Oh Liberty, what crimes are committed in thy name!)

– Madame Roland, to the clay statue of Liberty at the Place
de la Revolution, before placing her head
on the guillotine to be beheaded.
– Paris, 8 November 1793

The imbalance of power exercised in the absence of effective global governance institutions by powerful nations to the detriment of other nations must rank among the greatest causes of human suffering in the world today. The mutual provocations and intransigence that characterise relations between powerful nuclear powers must rank among the greatest threats to human existence.

Dedicated to the people of Egypt, Libya, Syria, and Ukraine
and to all those committed to the pursuit of
peace and justice among nations.

CONTENTS

PART I
Legal Framework

PART II
Selected Cases of Foreign Intervention in the Twenty-First Century

PART III
A New and Humane World Order

PREFACE

It is my sad but sincere hope that the journey into this book will offer coherent evidence that powerful Western Nations have knowingly acted to impede peace and progress in regions of the world in the first two decades of this twenty-first century. Come with me.

At the end of December 2019, public health officials in China announced that they were seeing cases of respiratory disease in the City of Wuhan in Hubei Province, that were unfamiliar. This disease was subsequently identified as a novel coronavirus disease.

By the first week in January 2020, the World Health Organisation (WHO) had activated its Incident Management Support Team in the Region and published disease outbreak news on the new virus. The publication contained information provided by China to the WHO about their observations of, and public health response to the cluster of infections, which at the time were only seen in Wuhan and had caused no deaths.

On 10 January 2020, WHO issued guidance to all countries on how to detect and manage the new disease. The guidance was based on the (at the time) current and evolving understanding of the disease.

Two days later, Chinese authorities released the genetic sequence of the novel coronavirus to the international community. The following day the first case of novel corona virus infection outside China was detected in Thailand.

On 14 January 2020, WHO officials noted a major development in the understanding of the disease: initial indications of human-to-human transmission.

On 20 – 21 January 2020, WHO experts from China and Western Pacific Regional Office visited Wuhan. On 22 January, WHO issued a statement confirming the existence of human-to-human transmission of the new disease in Wuhan, but noted that further observation was needed to properly understand factors and process of transmission.

The Director-General (DG) of WHO immediately convened an Emergency Committee to assess the International Public Health Impact of the new disease. Seven days later (three days earlier than the 10-day period required by WHO policy), the Emergency Committee reported back to the Director-General, with a recommendation that the new disease should be declared a Public Health Emergency of International Concern (PHEIC). A PHEIC declaration by the DG of WHO should be a trigger for national public health authorities in every country to activate their own emergency monitoring and management plans.

On 16 February, WHO visited China with an international delegation that included experts from Canada, Germany, Japan, Nigeria, Republic of Korea, Singapore, and United States. They visited facilities in four cities – including Beijing and Wuhan – and spoke with health workers, scientists, and public health officials.

It seems that most of January and February were spent observing the new disease, gaining an understanding of its modes of transmission and effects, and defining curative and preventive measures.

By April, the virus had spread globally and was killing people in nearly every country. The United States had become a hotspot for its transmission. As criticism grew of his erratic handing of the pandemic, the President of the United States began to attack China. Everyone was baffled by the President's attacks. All Countries understood that even in April 2020, global knowledge of the novel corona disease was sketchy and consequently, their own response plans were still fluid and changing with improvements in the understanding of the disease. Countries knew that it was unfair, with the benefit of hindsight, to expect China to have known, in the earliest days of the appearance of the disease, any more than what it shared with the WHO and indeed with the international community. But nobody spoke up against the accusations and increasingly bellicose attacks by the United States on China.

The President of the United States may feel entitled to do whatever it takes to secure his re-election. The world is entitled to count the costs of his actions.

As the pandemic spread, it exposed major shortcomings in the pandemic readiness of many Western Nations. In many countries, the health systems had been popular targets for government budget reductions during years of austerity budgets in the aftermath of the 2008 financial crisis. The pandemic also revealed that on the other end of the Spectrum was communist China, which seemed to have acted promptly and resolutely to get the virus under control and was the only country with surplus stocks of medical equipment essential to the prevention and management of the disease. The envy was palpable.

China's fate was sealed when it was perceived by the West to be using its stocks medical equipment to gain goodwill abroad. This infuriated Western Powers who likely considered the 'soft diplomacy' of handouts as their exclusive territory that was now being invaded by communist China.

For the first time since the United States exited the Iran Nuclear deal, Europe and the United States appeared to be once again united by a common *frenemy*. There was talk of a new a world order. China could not be allowed to attain global prominence let alone dominance. Global Supply chains must be re-shaped and made less dependent on an unpredictable Chinese power. Western companies should leave China. But where to?

To India, they said. *Even* Africa. Anywhere but China.

Japan announced a $2 billion fund to support companies that wanted to relocate from China. Western media hailed the move as a giant step in the decoupling from China. I laughed when I heard it, because $2 billion is a drop in the ocean of costs associated the disrupting established manufacturing capacity in China and setting it up in India and / or Africa, especially at a time when many Western companies would need $2 billion just to get through the third quarter of 2020. But as long as the announcement fed the anti-China propaganda, it did not matter if it was factually relevant.

The viciousness of the attacks on China in the wake of the novel coronavirus pandemic, and on Russia in 2014 onwards, demonstrate the unwritten rules that govern the aspirations and prosperity of Nations in the early 21st Century: forget the charter of the United Nations. Forget the universal declaration of equality and equal opportunity among nations. If a country is aligned with the United States and its allies, it might be permitted to achieve prosperity or even greatness. Countries that are not aligned with the US and its allies will never be permitted to achieve progress in strategic areas, regardless of their efforts and comparative advantages in the area. They shall be subjected to Mafia-style attacks until they are broken.

In typical fashion, the attacks on China were not limited to presidential threats. They were multi-pronged attacks using media propaganda, diplomatic pressure, (which included open support for violent protests in Hong Kong and for Taiwanese pro-independence efforts), military provocation (which included joint US-Australian naval drills in the South China Sea), and economic pressure (which included calls for China to pay financial reparations to compensate for the global cost of the pandemic).

Think about this: the United States, … the country that enslaved blacks, invaded and destroyed Iraq on phoney evidence and in direct violation of a United Nations Security Council directive, invaded and destroyed Lybia by wrongly exploiting a United Nations

Security Council resolution, destabilized Ukraine and Hong Kong … has never as much as apologised let alone paid for these damages. And now it was calling for another country to pay reparations for something of which it is merely *accused without evidence.*

The European Union is expected to speak up against such embarrassing behaviour from its long-time close ally – some would even say big brother, having committed its share of damage around the world. But it said nothing. In February 2019, it had announced a resolution for the payment of reparations to Africa for crimes against Africa during European colonialization. To date, nothing has happened.

On 29 May 2020, the Guardian newspaper in the United Kingdom published an article in its economics section, which provided, for those who did not already know, the root cause of the sustained attacks by the West on China. The article by Jeffrey Frankel was entitled *"Is China overtaking the US as a financial and economic power?"*, and opened with, *"The World Bank's International Comparison Program has just released its latest measures of price levels and GDP across 176 countries – and the results are striking. For the first time, the ICP finds that China's total real (inflation-adjusted) income is slightly larger than that of the US.,,,"*

Translation: China is now the world's largest economy.

As if to avoid general panic among segments of its readers, the article's sub-caption reads, *"Despite World Bank figures, the US remains far ahead of China in the metric that [actually] counts"*.

If the persecution of China exposed the candid determination of the United States and its allies never to allow a competing power to gain a significant and growing advantage, the manner in which it goes about weakening countries was exposed by events that started in the US city of Minnesota just three days before the Guardian article that announced China's rise to the number one position, and rapidly engulfed the United States before spreading to other OECD Nations.

Angry protests broke out in the streets of Minnesota when video emerged of the very public and cold-blooded execution of an unarmed black man by four white police officers. Within days, major cities in the US were experiencing large protests. The National Guard was called in to help local police end or at least control the protests.

The US President warned via Twitter that looters would be shot ("when the looting starts, the shooting starts", a phrase that was used in 1967 by Miami police Chief Walter Headley and sparked angry reactions from civil rights leaders at the time). He [the President] also warned that he would deploy the US Army into the streets if protests continued.

In the context of the internal politics in the United States of America, these two statements by the President will be seen as insensitive and unconstitutional ramblings of a man intent on dividing the country. In the international context, it is nothing less than a call for a radical review of foreign interventions by the United States throughout the 21st Century. Some of the worst conflicts of the 21st Century were either caused by or aggravated by US and European pressure on foreign governments to stop them from using armed forces to control violent disruptions. Disruptions that were conceivably caused or at least aided by the US and EU to influence the policies of foreign countries. In Ukraine and Egypt, interventions resulted in the abdication of the Presidents. In Syria and Hong Kong, interventions nearly brought the governments to their knees, but ultimately missed their objectives of regime change. In Libya, an armed intervention prevented the government from confronting an armed insurrection. The excuse given by the US and EU for their intervention in Libya and support for armed insurrectionists within the country was that they were preventing the Libyan government from using force against its own people. Supported by the US and its allies, the rebels eventually reached the capital, overthrew the government, and cast the country into a decade of chaos, war and bloodshed that continues until today.

Therefore, as the protests roll on in the United States and the self-appointed leader of the free world struggles to find a justification for using excessive armed force against its own citizens in its own streets, it is time to re-visit its actions in other countries' conflicts and reveal the true villains of the those conflicts.

For most of the twenty-first century (and the 100 years before it), Europe and the United States formed a strategic alliance that effectively shaped the world. They generously rewarded nations that agreed with them and punished those that disagreed. This partnership was shaken to its core when Donald Trump was elected president and started implementing his America First policy.

INTRODUCTION

DRIFTING APART

During his first year of office, President Donald Trump signalled that he did not want the United States to continue sharing its dominant position in the world with Europe. He called NATO obsolete, accused European countries of not pulling their own weight, pulled out of a key global environmental agreement, openly praised and supported Brexit (the withdrawal of the United Kingdom from the European Union), frequently criticised Europe's immigration policy and its approach to the migrant crisis, and put Europe on the alert by announcing plans to withdraw from their joint nuclear deal with Iran.

On 9 May 2018, the United States unilaterally withdrew from the agreement, formally known as the Joint Comprehensive Plan of Action (JCPOA), generally referred to as the Iran nuclear deal. The JCPOA is an international agreement that was reached in 2015 by the Islamic Republic of Iran with the five permanent members of the United Nations Security Council, plus Germany and the European Union. The objective of the agreement was to prevent Iran from becoming a nuclear power. Under its terms, Iran agreed, among other provisions, to significantly reduce its stockpiles of enriched uranium and gas centrifuges, limit its enrichment activities over the deal's fifteen-year period (called the sunset clause), and comply with a strict inspection and verification regime by the International Atomic Energy Agency (IAEA). In return, Iran would benefit from a suspension of economic sanctions by Europe and the United States.

In 2015, the basket of US sanctions against Iran included punitive measures from different pieces of legislation and involving different departments such as the Department of Commerce and the Department of Defence. One of them is the Iran Sanctions Act, which was passed in 1996 as the Iran and Libya Sanctions Act (ILSA). In 2006, it was extended and renamed the Iran Sanctions Act (ISA) following the redemption of Libya by the international community (it was mainly a redemption by Europe and the United States). In 2016, both the United States House of Representatives and the Senate voted to extend the ISA for ten years and sent it to President Barack Obama for signature. The President declined to sign but allowed the act to become law without presidential endorsement. His view was that with the JCPOA already signed in 2015, there was no need to continue extending the ISA.

Sanction acts allow the president to issue individual waivers on a case-by-case basis. The mechanism of suspension of sanctions, for example against Iran under the JCPOA, required the president to issue renewable waivers for each punitive measure. If a time-limited waiver expires and is not renewed, that punitive measure would automatically reactivate.

During his presidential campaign, Donald Trump promised to "scrap" the JCPOA if he was elected president, describing it as "the worst deal ever negotiated." He maintained this stance after taking office on 20 January 2017.

During his final months of office, President Obama instructed Secretary of State John Kerry to issue waivers for the ISA and other sanctions applicable to the JCPOA. ISA waivers are valid for 120 days. Other sanctions have different validities. For example, NDAA, IFCA, ITRA need to be renewed every 180 days. In 2017, President Trump signed the waiver renewals. At the same time, he issued new sanctions against Iran and warned signatories to the JCPOA that the United States would pull out unless provisions were modified to address the concerns of his administration. Those concerns included, among other issues, President Trump's belief that Iran's ballistic missile programme and its influence on events in the Middle East – which he considers to be malign – should be part of the agreement and that the sunset clause should be scrapped and the prohibition against nuclear activities made permanent.

In January 2018, there was widespread speculation about whether Trump would continue to sign new waivers. He did. But warned the JCPOA signatories that it was his final waiver and they had to propose modifications to the agreement before the ISA was up for renewal again on 12 June 2018.

From mid-January until mid-April, nothing seemed to be happening—at least nothing that was visible in the public domain. But then just weeks before the ISA deadline, the lull was broken by a flurry of diplomatic activity:

On 23 April, Emmanuel Macron travelled to Washington to convince the president not to pull out of the deal.

On 27 April, German Chancellor Angela Merkel travelled to Washington with a similar message. *The Atlantic* captioned: "Exit Macron, Enter Merkel."

On 6 May, it was the turn of then British Foreign Secretary Boris Johnson. He travelled to Washington DC to meet his US counterpart and also to explain the European position on the agreement to Americans through a number of media engagements. CNN noted, "Boris Johnson takes to Fox News in last-ditch effort to save Iran deal" (7 May 2018). The Foreign and Commonwealth Office tried to play down the perception of panic around the JCPOA and said on its website that the Secretary was in America to discuss "Iran, North Korea, Syria, and other major international issues."

Meanwhile, on 30 April, Israeli President Benjamin Netanyahu had weighed in, accusing Iran of lying about its nuclear program.

Netanyahu presented "a series of slides and photographs of documents that he said were drawn from a half-ton cache obtained by Israeli intelligence" as new evidence to support his claims. But Ollie Heinonen, the former chief inspector of the International Atomic Energy Agency (IAEA), maintained that the information was neither new nor incriminating. He said the material presented by Netanyahu was known to the IAEA as early as 2005, and experts of the watchdog had satisfied themselves that the related program had been deactivated. The director general of the IAEA also confirmed that Iran was complying with its obligations under the JCPOA. He said, "We are concentrating on discharging our responsibility, which is to verify and monitor Iran's implementation of its nuclear-related commitments under the JCPOA.

As I have said many times, I believe the JCPOA represents a significant gain for verification. The IAEA now has the world's most robust verification regime in place in Iran. We have had access to all the locations that we needed to visit.

Our inspection work has doubled since 2013. IAEA inspectors now spend three thousand calendar days per year on the ground in Iran. We have installed some two thousand tamper-proof seals on nuclear material and equipment.

We have carried out more than sixty complementary accesses and visited more than 190 buildings since JCPOA Implementation Day.

We collect and analyse hundreds of thousands of images captured daily by our sophisticated surveillance cameras in Iran—about half the total images that we collect throughout the world.

We collect over one million pieces of open source information each month.

All of our activities are supported by state-of-the-art technology, including data collecting and processing systems. Our current verification capability is much stronger than it has ever been.

As of today, I can state that Iran is implementing its nuclear-related commitments. It is essential that it continues to do so. If the

JCPOA were to fail, it would be a great loss for nuclear verification and for multilateralism".

The declarations of the IAEA addressed the Israeli accusations. As a member of the IAEA, Israel must have been aware of the information provided by IAEA officials in response to its accusations against Iran. Therefore, either the Israeli President was lying, or the Director General of the IAEA was.

Regardless, Israel has nuclear weapons. As such, it has no right to complain against other countries owning or aspiring to own them. It is normal for countries that are fundamentally opposed to nuclear weapons to demand of those that own them to decommission and demand of those that aspire to own them to desist. But when a country that owns nuclear weapons and has no intention of decommissioning is shouting at aspiring countries, it is evidence of prevalence of the law of the powerful, by the powerful, and for the powerful.

In any case, the IAEA did not address US concerns regarding Iran's long-range ballistic missiles, the sunset clause, or Iran's regional role. Instead, it clarified that it is only responsible for monitoring the nuclear aspects of the agreement, and that any other issues outside the nuclear aspects must be addressed by the various governments.

The view from Europe and Iran was that there was nothing to address. As far they were concerned, treaty was still valid and all signatories – except, of course, the United States – were fully compliant.

On 8 May 2018, President Donald Trump announced that the JCPOA signatories had not made the modifications he demanded while issuing the January 2018 waivers, and as a result, he would not renew the waivers.

European leaders were shocked. As the reality of the US decision sank in, shock transformed into a quiet resolve to uphold the treaty in the wake of and in defiance of the American decision.

Germany, France, and the United Kingdom issued a joint statement expressing their commitment to the agreement.

In a statement to the British House of Commons, Foreign Secretary Johnson said that the government "regrets the decision of the US administration to withdraw from the deal and to re-impose American sanctions on Iran." He urged America to "avoid taking any action that would hinder other parties from continuing to make the agreement work in the interests of our collective national security." He also said on Twitter that the "UK remains strongly committed to the JCPOA and will work with E3 partners and the other parties to the deal to maintain it."

French President Macron was keen to find a way to get the Americans back on board. He said, "We will work collectively on a broader framework, covering nuclear activity, the post-2025 period, ballistic activity, and stability in the Middle East, notably Syria, Yemen, and Iraq."

His foreign minister, Jean-Yves Le Drian, added that European foreign ministers will meet with Iranian officials to discuss options for the future of the JCPOA (Al Jazeera: "World Leaders React to US Withdrawal from Iranian Nuclear Deal," 9 May 2018).

In 2017, Europe was consolidating its business interests in Iran, fully aware of the risk of the US pulling out of the JCPOA. It is not clear what contingency plans they put in place to mitigate against an American withdrawal. What is clear is that European leaders knew that the probability was high, not least because the US president had said it repeatedly, and by every indication, European leaders were taking his words seriously.

At a Europe-Iran forum held in Zurich in October 2018, Helga Schmidt, Secretary General of the European External Action Service told business leaders that the EU was committed to the JCPOA and would do everything to make sure that it stays (Saeed Kamali Dehghan, "Europe's Business Heads Aim to Keep Iran Nuclear Deal Despite US Threat," theguardian.com, 6 October 2017). European businesses interested in Iran opportunities were concerned about deficiencies in banking infrastructure, with major banks still reluctant to handle Iranian transactions. Schmidt gave assurances that "as a sign of confidence in our future financial and economic relations, the European commission has proposed to allow the European Investment Bank operating in Iran in the future."

Economic Interests Dominating International Agreements

In the immediate aftermath of the US withdrawal in May 2018, European leaders were emphasising the importance of the JCPOA to global security and the sanctity of international agreements as the reason for their defence of the agreement. Meanwhile, the media was suggesting that this was not the entire picture and highlighted the underlying economic stakes.

CNBC: "Europe moves to safeguard Iran interests after US pullout" (11 May 2018).

Reuters: "France to do utmost to protect business interests in Iran" (9 May 2018) In this article, Reuters claims that: "French exports to Iran doubled in 2017 to 1.5 billion euros ($1.78 billion), driven by the export of jets and aircraft parts, as well as automobile parts, according to customs data. Total trade between France and Iran hit a nine-year high last year of 3.8 billion euros."

It is clear from the article that the interests of French businesses were playing an important role in shaping the foreign policy priorities and actions. According to the article, the French Foreign Minister made clear that France will "obviously do everything, in conjunction with [its] businesses, to protect their interests."

Daily Star: "France Wants to Protect Business Interests in Iran: Elysee Source" (9 May 2018).

The Jerusalem Post: "France Wants to Protect Business Interests in Iran." (9 May 2018)

Reuters: "France's Finance Minister Bruno Le Maire said EU states would propose sanctions-blocking measures to the European Commission. 'Do we accept extraterritorial sanctions? The answer is no,' Le Maire told reporters. 'Do we accept that the United States is the economic gendarme of the planet? The answer is no. Do we accept the vassalization of Europe in commercial matters? The answer is no'" (Paul Carrel, Leigh Thomas, "Europe Moves to Safeguard Interests in Iran after US Pullout," Reuters, 11 May 2018).

Dear readers, hands up those who believe that prior to May 2018, France and Europe acted, alone or in concert with the United States, to impose extraterritorial sanctions (Libya, Ukraine). Hands up those who believe that France and Europe acted as the economic gendarme of the planet and led the vassalization of their postcolonial territories in all matters, not just commercial. Hands up those who still believe that Europe and United States interventions in other countries are driven by humanitarian rather than economic interests.

ABC News (citing the Associated Press): "A group representing German trade interests says the U.S. decision to withdraw from the Iran nuclear deal will hit Germany's economy hard.... Eric Schweitzer [head of the Association of German Chambers of Commerce and Industry] ... urged Germany's government and the European Union to protect German business interests."

The Hill: "For Europe, the Iran nuclear deal is all about trade" (Sandeep Gopalan, 7 May 2018).

Conflict of Interests

What we are seeing here is a dangerous and unregulated mixing of national business interests with international security and humanitarian agreements. This introduces huge risks of conflict of interests and distortions to fair competition. Incidentally, Western media and experts reported the pressure of European business on their governments as a matter of fact. None of the articles expressed concerns about a conflict of interest or unfair competition.

Unfair competition: governments use their place at the negotiating table of global issues to create markets for their domestic companies, which amounts to a state subsidy.

Conflict of interest: The mixing of national economic interest with issues of regional security and humanitarianism is unethical, potentially fraught with corruption and raises serious questions about the real objectives. The mere perception of the involvement of selfish economic interests can be enough to undermine the legitimacy of an intervention and create discontent.

Double standards

In the build-up to the Ukraine crisis in 2013, Russia repeatedly expressed concerns that a Deep Comprehensive Trade Agreement between the European Union and Ukraine would harm Russia's economic interests in Ukraine. European Union officials ridiculed those concerns with statements like 'Russia has no exclusive claim over Ukraine'.

This book asserts that when the European Union forced itself into a DCTA with Ukraine, it impacted Russian Economic interests in much the same way as European interests were impacted by the United States forcing its way out of the JCPOA with Iran.

In this section, we see the European Union asserting its right to act in any way necessary to defend its economic interests in the wake of the unilateral withdrawal by the United States from the JCPOA, In Chapter 9, we see the European Union criticizing and delegitimizing Russia's moves to act in any way necessary to protect its interests in Ukraine in the wake of the interference by the European Union.

Anger in Europe

With so much at stake over the Iran JCPOA, it is understandable that the European leaders' attempts at gentle dissuasion soon turned to anger, criticism, and defiance when Donald Trump announced his decision to abandon the agreement.

Merkel: "If everybody does what they like, then this is bad news for the world."

Le Drian: "We feel that the extraterritoriality of their sanction measures are unacceptable. The Europeans should not have to pay for the withdrawal from an agreement by the United States" (bbc.com, "Iran Nuclear Deal: France Condemns US Move to Re-Impose Sanctions," 11 May 2018).

Financial Times (opinion piece): "This is not the first time Europeans have been confronted with Mr Trump's disdain for an international order that used to underwrite US global leadership. America First has seen him quit the Paris climate change accord, jettison the idea of a two-state solution to the Israel-Palestine conflict, tear up trade agreements and question the NATO alliance. Then there are the Twitter fusillades accusing Europe of being soft on terrorists or tolerating imaginary no-go areas of Muslim migrants. The allies for the most part have kept their counsel.

The exit from the Iran deal is different. It marks the biggest rupture in transatlantic relations since the end of the cold war and mocks the West's efforts to uphold a rules-based order. It surrenders the international high ground to a deeply unpleasant regime in Tehran. And it pours petrol on a region already in flames. A region, incidentally, that sits alongside Europe" (Philip Stevens: "How Europe Should React to Donald Trump," ft.com, 10 May 2018).

The German chancellor's concerns that everyone doing whatever they like with impunity is bad for the world are fully justified. The French foreign minister is also right in his assessment that it is not fair to expect Europe to pay the price for the policy decisions of the United States.

As Europe complains bitterly against the flouting of international law and norms by the United States (still a close ally despite the many and growing differences), the moment is propitious to reflect on aspects of the international leadership of both Europe and the United States over the past two decades, particularly foreign interventions. A leadership that has been characterized by a singular focus on defending and furthering their common interests, often in blatant disregard for international law and with great harm to other nations.

First, a brief review of the legal framework that governs or should govern relations between countries.

PART I

LEGAL FRAMEWORK

This section describes the main aspects of the laws that govern international relations. This will provide some perspective to the discussion of foreign interventions in subsequent sections.

Some experts argue that international laws are incomplete. Most experts agree that as with the legislations of most countries, international law, while imperfect, is currently fit for its purpose and the problem is a lack of implementation rather than inadequacy.

CHAPTER 1

SOURCES OF INTERNATIONAL LAW

The International Court of Justice (ICJ) is charged with the development and exercise of the framework for international law, and its statute states that it shall do so based on treaties, customary international law, and general principles of law, as well as, in some cases, judicial decisions and expert opinions.

Decisions by institutions such as the United Nations General Assembly and the United Nations Security Council provide other sources of international law. Although they are not included in the statute of the ICJ, these sources are influential. But they are also incoherent and controversial. Some resolutions of the UN Security Council are binding, and other resolutions in identical circumstances are nonbinding recommendations. Of those resolutions that are binding, some are enforced militarily, while others are not. Whether a binding resolution is enforced or not depends on several factors, such as underlying interests of the members of the Security Council.

The Law of Treaties

A treaty is an international agreement between states in written form and forming part of international law.

The main instrument governing the generation and execution of treaties today is the Vienna Convention of 1969.

The Secretary General of the United Nations is the main depository of multilateral treaties. More than 560 multilateral treaties are currently held by the UN, as well as tens of thousands of other treaties registered by states.

The UN Charter is one of the treaties that forms the basis of international law.

Customary International Law

Customary international law is based not on written and signed agreements but on state practice – a collection of rules that have been generally accepted by most countries. To qualify as international law, a state practice of commission or omission must be consistent and uniform, of a certain duration, and generally accepted among nations as law.

International Humanitarian Law

The treaty basis of international humanitarian law is provided by the Geneva Convention of 1949 and associated protocols, plus other treaties and protocols.

Customary international law is based on a collection of rules that have been generally accepted by most countries.

International Human Rights Law

The framework of international human rights law is provided by the International Bill of Human Rights, which was constituted by the Universal Declaration of Human Rights issued in December 1948. It is the international covenant on human, political, economic, social, and cultural rights.

State Sovereignty and Non-Intervention

The concept of state sovereignty embodies the ideas that a state has complete and exclusive control over its territory, people and resources; that all states are equal regardless of their geographic size, population, and economic or military might; and that no state shall have the right to tell another state how to run its internal affairs. State sovereignty is also called Westphalian sovereignty, after the Treaty of Westphalia, which ended the Thirty-Years' War in 1648. There is some debate among scholars as to whether this treaty actually established the notion of states. However, most people agree that the basic form of sovereign states emerged from the Westphalia Treaty.

The basis for state sovereignty in contemporary international law is provided by the Charter of the United Nations. Article 2(4) prohibits attacks on the "political independence and territorial integrity" of states, and Article 2(7) contains further restrictions on intervention.

International Rule of Law among Nations

The concept of international rule of law among nations results from the concepts of state sovereignty and non-intervention. This means that within the international commonwealth of Nations, each sovereign state is entitled to expect and receive the same assurances of equality before the law and equal penalties for similar violations, in much the same way as individual citizens within sovereign states.

Although international law ascribes rights, obligations, and restrictions to individual sovereign states, it does not create an international sovereign power to enforce the laws. In the absence of an international sovereign, individual sovereign states have assumed enforcement rights that, ironically, often violate the same international laws and norms they claim to enforce.

Summary of Key Provisions of International Law

Sovereignty of states: article 2(1) of the UN Charter says the organisation is based on the principle of sovereign equality of all its members.

Peaceful settlement of disputes: article 2(7) of the UN Charter says all members shall settle their international disputes by peaceful means in such a manner that international peace and security as well as justice are not endangered.

International interventions: article 39 of the UN Charter says the Security Council shall determine the existence of any threat to the peace, breach of the peace, or act of aggression and shall make recommendations for, or decide, what measures shall be taken in accordance with articles 41 and 42 to maintain or restore international peace and security.

Article 46 of the UN Charter says plans for the application of armed force shall be made by the Security Council with the assistance of the Military Staff Committee.

Geneva Conventions: protection of prisoners of war.

Customary rules of the international humanitarian law: protection of civilians in armed conflict, with no protection for armed combatants.

CHAPTER 2

INTERNATIONAL LAW JUSTIFICATION OF INTERVENTIONS

The emergence of international humanitarian law (IHL), the development of international human rights law, and globalisation are changing the absolute and exclusive prerogative of sovereign states. International humanitarian law respects the sovereignty of states over their citizens but adds a responsibility to protect citizens from genocide, ethnic cleansing, and crimes against humanity, according to the International Commission on Intervention and State Sovereignty (ICISS). It provides that where a sovereign state is either unable or unwilling to provide such protection to its own cotozens, the international community has the responsibility to protect (RtoP) the affected citizens of that country.

In essence therefore, IHL is the collective voice of modern humanity saying, "we will not be passive witnesses to extreme suffering under the pretext of respecting state sovereignty".

Western governments frequently use this provision of IHL and the abhorrence of foreign dictatorships by their citizens to legitimize foreign interventions. Neither the governments nor the media care to explain that IHL also specifies that humanitarian interventions must be led by the UNSC, and that nations who violate these provisions are themselves dictatorships.

Some nations have been quick to interpret RtoP as suspension of the sovereignty of the state. Others have exploited it for their own national ambitions. However, the United Nations has been very clear that the primary objective of RtoP is to provide support to the sovereign state. The UN defines three principal pillars by which this should be done: supporting the struggling state to help it meet its responsibility by itself, intervening through peaceful means, and intervening through armed forces. There is an ongoing debate about whether these three should be applied sequentially. In any case, armed intervention must be sanctioned and led by the United Nations Security Council (UNSC).

Civilians' Loss of Right to Protection

Under international humanitarian law, civilians who are actively involved in hostilities of conflict are not eligible for protection under RtoP.

Controversial Cases of Intervention

In 2003, the United States and its allies launched a military invasion of Iraq. The intervention was not sanctioned by the United Nations Security Council. The United States and Great Britain justified their actions by citing their right to self-defence, claiming that Iraq posed a "grave and gathering" danger with its weapons of mass destruction. Article 51 of the United Nations Charter gives member states a right to self-defense, but only in the event of an attack, and only for so long until the UN Security Council has taken measures to normalize the situation or remain in control of it.

A grave and gathering danger does not constitute an attack and therefore does not justify the use of force in self-defense.

Many experts and governments disagreed with the assessment by the United States and Great Britain that Iraq posed any threat to the security of the United States or of world, let alone an imminent threar. In the end, it was proven that Iraq did not have weapons of mass destruction. Even if they had such weapons, there was no proof beyond doubt that they were imminently going to deploy them against the United States.

In 2011, the United States, Britain, France, and their allies launched a military intervention in Libya, claiming to be enforcing United Nations Security Council resolutions 1970 and 1973. They later handed the command to NATO. United Nations Resolution 1973 authorised the use of "all possible means" to establish an immediate ceasefire and protect civilians in Libya. By the time Resolution 1973 was passed on 17 March 2011, there was a civil war in Libya. It is not clear what, if any, measures the intervention took to directly protect civilians. The intervention violated the calls for an immediate ceasefire by providing extensive support to armed rebel combatants.

CHAPTER 3

PAST RULINGS ON FOREIGN INTERVENTION (JURISPRUDENCE)

On 9 April 1986, the Republic of Nicaragua filed an international lawsuit against the United States of America at the International Court of Justice in connection with "military and paramilitary activities in and against Nicaragua." The ruling of the International Court of Justice on this issue, passed on 27 June 1986, was a landmark case in international law. In that ruling, the ICJ

- rejected the justification of collective self-defence put forward by the United States for actions;
- decided that by training, arming, equipping, financing, and supplying the Contra forces or otherwise encouraging, supporting, and aiding military and paramilitary activities in and against Nicaragua, America acted against the Republic of Nicaragua in breach of America's obligation under customary international law not to intervene in the affairs of another state;
- decided that the United States of America, by certain attacks on Nicaraguan territory from 1983 to 1984, had acted against the Republic of Nicaragua in breach of its obligation under

customary international law not to use force against another state;

- decided that the United States of America, by directing or authorising overflights of Nicaraguan territory, had acted against the Republic of Nicaragua in breach of its obligation under customary international law not to violate the sovereignty of another state;

- found that the United States of America, by producing in 1983 a manual entitled *Sicológicas en Guerra de Guerrillas* and disseminating it to Contra forces [Nicaraguan Rebels], had encouraged the commission by them of acts contrary to general principles of humanitarian law (but did not find a basis for concluding that their acts were imputable to the United States of America);

- decided that the United States of America, by the attacks on Nicaraguan territory and by declaring a general embargo on trade with Nicaragua on 1 May 1985, had committed acts calculated to deprive the purpose of the Treaty of Friendship, Commerce, and Navigation between the parties signed at Managua on 21 January 1956; and

- decided that the United States of America was under an obligation to make reparation to the Republic of Nicaragua for all injury caused to Nicaragua by the breaches of obligations under customary international law enumerated above.

Since the ICJ passed this landmark ruling in 1986, the USA, European Union, individual European Countries and NATO have carried out similar interventions in other countries either jointly or individually, covertly and openly.

CHAPTER 4

NATIONAL INTERESTS VERSUS INTERNATIONAL RULE OF LAW

Many great empires and civilisations were built by simply invading wealthy states with weak defences. The case of Nicaragua versus the United States of America showed that this was still very much the case in the mid–1980s.

The ruling of the ICJ in the matter had a profound effect. However, most observers agree that it did not effectively end the practice of interest-driven interventions. Nations continue to face pressures to seek solutions to their own economic and political issues through intervention in other countries, albeit it with increased effort to legitimise their actions using the provisions of international law.

As nations grow, they need energy and resources to sustain their growth and access to markets for their goods and services. As more countries strive for growth and prosperity, the competition for resources and markets (which by definition are finite) grows more intense. Conflicts develop when interests in these areas collide.

In theory, access to raw materials and markets for finished goods and services should be regulated by mechanisms of free trade. In practice, however, competition for access to both raw materials and markets is so intense, and developed countries so perilously dependent on them, that they cannot afford to leave the fate of their countries to free trade mechanisms or even to the sovereign decisions of non-allied nations.

In the years 2000 to 2001, the state of California experienced severe power outages that affected millions of people for several days. On 16 May 2001, a task force set up by President George W. Bush concluded and recommended, among other issues, that energy security must become a key driver of US foreign policy. Two years later, the United States led the invasion of oil-rich Iraq, deposed its leader, and facilitated transition to a pro-US regime. In the wake of the invasion, Western companies won lucrative oil and gas deals in Iraq.

By the end of the first decade of the twenty-first century, NATO was facing questions over its continued relevance in a post-Cold War world. At a strategic concept summit in Lisbon on 19–20 November 2010 that was billed as the most important in its history, NATO pointed out that all of its members were extremely vulnerable to potential disruptions to their energy supplies. It redefined its mission as safeguarding the energy supplies of its members. Four months later, it launched a controversial military intervention in a cash- and oil-rich country at Europe's doorsteps [Libya].

PART II

SELECTED CASES OF FOREIGN INTERVENTION IN THE TWENTY-FIRST CENTURY

CHAPTER 5

THE ARAB SPRING

The term "Arab Spring" refers to uprisings that took place in several countries of North Africa and the Middle East in the spring of 2011 and is used interchangeably to describe the events, the ideas they engendered, the movement, and the period in which they occurred. The most prominent uprisings took place in Bahrain, Tunisia, Egypt, Libya, Syria, and Yemen. There were smaller (or perhaps just less widely reported) unrests in other countries such as Morocco and Saudi Arabia.

By many accounts, the Arab Spring started on 17 December 2010 in Tunisia, where a street vendor called Mohamed Bouazizi set himself on fire after his merchandise was confiscated. This incident sparked widespread protests all over Tunisia. Initially, people were protesting high unemployment, high prices, corruption, and lack of political freedoms in solidarity with Bouazizi. But their demands later turned to calls for the president's resignation. The president hung on for a few weeks and battled the protests, but he finally resigned on 14 January 2011. By this time, the protests had already spread to Egypt and other countries.

Arab Spring demonstrations in North Africa were characterised by large gatherings in popular squares and extensive use of social media for planning, coordination, and publicity. In most countries, the movement had no clear leader. Demonstrations started out peacefully but almost always turned violent and aggressive. They received vocal support from Western leaders, who issued stern warnings to authorities to exercise restraint. The Arab Spring was covered extensively by both conventional media and social media.

The main criticism I have for media coverage of the Arab Spring is that, along with Western governments, they covered up the atrocities of the demonstrators. It is important to note that the United States and Europe also experience violent and disruptive protests, and the response of governments is always very clear: stern, resolute force. Governments always insist that all protests must be registered in advance and only proceed if approved and in strict accordance with the conditions of approval. Governments always remind citizens that while they have a constitutional right to express themselves without fear of harassment, they also have a civic obligation to respect the rule of law and the rights of other citizens to go about their daily business uninhibited. A good example is the dispersal of the Occupy Wall Street movement in New York City in November 2011. Responding to the appeals of the protesters, New York City's mayor released a statement saying, "No right is absolute and with every right comes responsibilities. The First Amendment gives every New Yorker the right to speak out. But it does not give anyone the right to sleep in a park or otherwise take it over to the exclusion of others—nor does it permit anyone in our society to live outside the law. There is no ambiguity in the law here; the First Amendment protects speech—it does not protect the use of tents and sleeping bags to take over a public space."

Therefore, policies of Western governments to provide unreserved support to violent and disruptive protests represent at best a lack of consistency in policy (double standards) and at worst a systematic, calculated use of disruptive street protests to achieve controversial policy objectives (regime change). The latter opinion is strengthened by a strong correlation between support for disruptive protests and Western regime change policy. Western governments and media provided strong support and protection to disruptive protests in Egypt, armed rebels in Libya, and armed protests in Ukraine. Western governments had demonstrably strong interest in regime change in all three countries. Western governments and media looked the other way when Saudi troops crossed the causeway and dispersed Arab Spring demonstrators in Manama, the capital of Bahrain. Western governments had demonstrably strong interest in the preservation of leadership in Bahrain.

In general, the Arab Spring failed to deliver the lasting change that the campaigners had hoped for. Many of the countries settled back into their pre-protest status quo:

In Tunisia, the resignation of the president was followed by a period of relative calm, although unfortunately, the calm was occasionally broken by devastating terrorist attacks.

In Bahrain, the intervention of Saudi army effectively ended the protests.

In Morocco, the king announced sweeping constitutional reforms; Morocco stayed true to its image as a model for progressive monarchy and stability in North Africa.

In Egypt, the initial euphoria that greeted the resignation of long-time ruler Hosni Mubarak quickly turned into a period of turmoil and upheaval that saw thousands of people killed and tens of thousands imprisoned. Egypt had four presidents in two years and still ended up where it had started: an autocratic military leader turned civilian and ruthless crackdowns on the press and on social liberties (see the next chapter).

In Libya, the movement quickly turned into an armed insurgency. There is a possibility that it always was an armed insurgency but disguised itself as civilian protests in its initial stages. Whatever its true nature, the insurgency overthrew Muammar Gaddafi, the long-time military ruler, with military support from a coalition led by Europe and the United States. The country was devastated by the fighting; it degenerated into chaos in 2011, and today (2020), it remains a failed state, with two rival governments, both incapable of fixing the destructive legacy of the insurgency. The country is rife with tribal conflict, terrorist camps, and a thriving human trafficking and slave trade. Far from holding to account the governments that led the invasion, Western media has conveniently kept this ugly legacy and the daily suffering it causes to the people of Africa out of the living rooms of Western TV audiences.

In Syria, Western governments found regime change via proxies a lot more difficult (see chapter 8).

CHAPTER 6

THE ARAB SPRING: HOW IT HAPPENED IN EGYPT

Just when things were beginning to calm down in Tunisia, they were picking up in Egypt. Three days after the Tunisian president resigned, an Egyptian man set himself on fire outside the parliament building in Cairo to protest government repression. People took to the streets to express solidarity with this act, and protests soon spread to other cities.

As the protests spread, the crowds grew angrier and clashed frequently with the forces of law and order. Thousands of people camped out in public squares around the clock. The largest gatherings were around Tahrir Square.

The cost of providing food and refreshments for the protesters is not known but is likely to be in the millions of dollars. (It would be interesting to understand how it was funded; follow the money).

As Egypt was preparing to observe a national holiday on 25 January 2011 in honour of police forces, protest organisers used social media to call on Egyptians to take to the streets on the same day for what they called a "day of rage."

The decision to hold the protests on Police Commemoration Day would be a cause for concern to those who are passionate about rights of people to express themselves freely and peacefully. There is nothing wrong in protesting on such a day, but responsible protest leaders must weigh the benefits of exposure and publicity against the risk of clashes in the potentially tense atmosphere that is inevitable due protocol and security requirements on such days. The decision of the organisers to call their protests a "day of rage" is also an indication that the organizers did not intend their demonstrations to be peaceful. It is difficult to visualize a day of rage ending peacefully.

At this point, Western governments and Western media should have been picking up on this and calling out the protesters to express themselves calmly and peacefully, consistent with the message they always send to demonstrators in their own countries. The fact they did not do this is regrettable. The fact they kept referring to the protests as peaceful is at best misguided but potentially slightly more sinister. There is nothing peaceful about a day of rage.

Al Jazeera reported that the first few hours of the protests were calm, after which protesters and police began to clash. It is not clear how the clashes began, or which side provoked them. What is clear is that after a few hours, the protests were no longer peaceful. This may appear to be a minute detail, but it is not. It is fundamental to understanding the role of Western governments in the Arab Spring. Europe and the United States have zero-tolerance policies, within their own countries, for protests that clash with law enforcement. Europe and the United States both openly supported the protesters even after the outbreak of clashes and exerted a high amount of pressure on the Egyptian government as it attempted to deal with the situation. Western governments were forcing the Egyptian government to treat the disruptive protests as if they were peaceful protests. This is the essential ingredient that enabled the protests to grow, incapacitate the government and ultimately topple it.

This use of excessive diplomatic pressure represents a violation of the principle of non-intervention in the affairs of sovereign states, which is anchored both in international law and in the UN Charter.

But it was justified by the urgent need to defend the rights to peaceful expression. If the protests were not peaceful—and they were not—there are serious questions to be asked of Western governments.

Unfortunately, the media was not asking those questions. Even if the protests had been peaceful, important questions must still be asked. Europe and the United States have no right or obligation to play global sheriff, judge, and police. Matters between states must be handled by the correct international institutions, just as matters between citizens must be handled by the relevant competent courts.

During the Cairo clashes, protesters attacked the police with rocks and firebombs, and police responded with tear gas and water cannons. This continued through the next day, with protests intensifying. In Washington DC, Hillary Clinton, the Secretary of State for the United States, said the Egyptian government should view the protests as an opportunity for "political, economic and social reforms to respond to the legitimate needs and interests of the Egyptian people." Secretary Clinton further said that the Egyptian government "should not prevent peaceful protests."[10] Quite importantly, the secretary's statement did not include an unequivocal call for the protesters to be peaceful or respect the forces of law and order or refrain from violence.

The significance of this statement in the context of equality of nations and non-intervention in the affairs of sovereign states cannot be overemphasised. The United States has serious problems related to human and civil rights issues. During celebrations of Martin Luther King Jr. Day in the 2018, many commentators agreed that Dr. King would be disappointed at the state of race relations in the United States today. The Egyptian government does not lecture (let alone pressurise) the US government on the treatment of African Americans, and it is not for lack of reason to do so but out of respect for US sovereignty.

The day following the comments from the US State Department, Mohamed Elbaradei arrived in Cairo to participate in the protests, saying he was "ready to lead the transition if asked to."

In the build-up to the Iraq War, Elbaradei was the head of the International Atomic Energy Agency. His agency was responsible for carrying out inspections in Iraq and providing assurance to the United Nations and the international community that Iraq complied with its obligations and did not pose a nuclear threat to the world. Instead, its inspectors never seemed to establish a sustainable working relationship with the government of Saddam Hussein. Some missions were ended prematurely, with inspectors complaining that they had not been given "full and unfettered" access to all relevant sites. Of course, the Iraqi government always claimed quite the opposite and expressed frustration at the agency and its inspectors.

Before the vote on the UN resolution for military intervention in Iraq, the IAEA said that it should be given more time to complete its ongoing work there. But the United States refused.

Now, Elbaradei was a citizen, looking to play a role in what he saw as an imminent transition in Egypt.

In Cairo, demonstrations continued, with increasing levels of violence. Protesters set the headquarters of the NDP Party on fire. The NDP (National Democratic Party), was the ruling party headed by President Mubarak. It was founded in 1978 by President Anwar El Sadat.

The government escalated the security measures by implementing a curfew and limiting access to mobile data services and social media. By this time, protesters had already set up a tent village on Tahrir Square, and the new security measures did little to deter them. Protesters simply remained camped out on Tahrir Square, occasionally clashing with police. On 29 January 2011, President Mubarak appeared on television and dismissed the government. The following day, he appointed a vice president. This was Egypt's first vice president in Mubarak's (nearly) thirty-year rule.

On 1 February 2011, exactly five days after Elbaradei's talk of the transition, Mubarak announced that he would not seek re-election when his current term of office ended in September 2011.

In the aftermath of the announcement, the level of violence in the streets intensified as Mubarak supporters poured into the streets and clashed with anti-government protesters.

As the events were unfolding in Egypt, the official position of Western governments was that Egyptians were in charge of their own destiny. At one point, US officials said, "We cannot decide the future of Egypt. That must be done by the Egyptians themselves." (www. voanews.com, "US Senators Speak out on Egypt", 31 January 2011)

This was far from the truth. We now know from various sources that far away from the streets of Cairo, intense political activity at the highest levels of the US government was shaping both current events in Egypt and its future leadership. The media knew this but continued to promote the narrative of the US government: that Egyptians were controlling their own destiny.

Similarly, we now know that, as events were unfolding in the streets of Ukraine two years later, officials of the US State Department were plotting the shape of the future leadership of Ukraine behind the scenes. The media was aware of this but maintained their anti-Russia narratives.

In 2016, five years after the Arab Spring, *The Financial Times* revealed in a wide-ranging article that during the Egyptian uprising the US government wanted regime change in Cairo and was working behind the scenes to achieve it (Financial Times, "Clinton and Obama: An American Rift over an Egyptian Despot," 27 October 2016) According to the article, on 31 January 2011, the US government sent Frank Wisner, a former American ambassador, to meet with Mubarak in Cairo, warn him against using violence against protesters, and ask him to start mapping out a political transition. Meanwhile, other back channels were also being tried. "Michael Morrel, deputy head of the CIA, was approached by an Egyptian contact who claimed to be speaking on behalf of Omar Suleiman, Egypt's intelligence chief, who had been named vice-president that week by Mr. Mubarak. He appeared to be asking what [they] needed to do to keep the US [on their side]. Mr. Morell [replied] to his contact on February 1 with 'some specific commitments' about Mr. Mubarak stepping down. He [Mr. Morell] was told [by his contact] that Mr. Suleiman agreed with the ideas and had convinced Mr. Mubarak to announce them that day. But when the Egyptian leader appeared on television, the agreed points were not mentioned. Instead, [he said], 'The events of the past few days impose on us the choice between chaos and stability.'"

When President Obama heard Mubarak's announcement, he is said to have been "exasperated" and replied, "That is not enough. That is just not going to do it." The atmosphere in the White House was intense.

Obama called Mubarak and spent thirty minutes on the telephone, trying to pressure him to step down immediately. An angry Mubarak responded, "You naïve Americans. You do not realise how this society would come apart if I were to walk away." Both the defence and foreign secretaries seemed to agree.

The Financial Times reported, "When Obama told his team in the Situation Room after the call [with Mubarak] that he intended to make a statement about Egypt, the dispute broke out again. Bob Gates, the Defence Secretary, … was the strongest opposing voice, warning the US should not encourage a swift transition when it had no idea what would follow."

Continued *The Financial Times*, "Mrs. Clinton instinctively took a more subtle tack. While the US should deliver tough messages in private, she was worried about the reaction among allies in the Gulf if it looked as if the administration was eager to force Mr. Mubarak out. President Obama agreed with Mrs. Clinton that the US should encourage an 'orderly transition' but said Egypt would become more unstable if violence continued. It was time to give Mr. Mubarak a bigger public nudge."

Despite the caution of his most senior diplomat, the following day, the president went ahead with his speech, which called on Mubarak to leave immediately. "Meaningful change must start now," he said.

"Mr. Obama's statement left some ambiguity about how the transition should unfold," *The Financial Times* reported, "but Robert Gibbs, the White House press secretary, was more emphatic the following day. Asked when the transition should start, he said 'now started yesterday.'"

Apart for the political activity within the US administration, discussions were being held with the Saudis and the Israelis about what would be best for the region.

Washington's allies were already unsettled by the criticism of Mr. Mubarak, but after the Gibbs comment, the phones started to ring.

The Saudis, including the late King Abdullah, insisted that the US should stand by Mubarak. Israel was also deeply worried about what would come next. Sheikh Mohammed bin Zayed, the crown prince of Abu Dhabi, warned that Egypt could become "a Sunni version of Iran."[11]

On 11 February 2011, President Mubarak bowed to the pressure from Washington, announced his resignation, and left Cairo. The Supreme Council of the Armed Forces (SCAF) took over control of the country and announced that it would only be in power for six months, during which time it would write a new constitution, organise parliamentary and presidential elections, and hand over power to a civilian government. It also pledged to respect all international treaties, including the 1979 peace treaty with Israel.

After Mubarak's resignation, the protesters on Tahrir Square declared victory. To them, it was finally "Egypt First!" Unfortunately, their enthusiasm faded as the weeks went by. It was not Egypt First. It was "America and Europe First."

Without a doubt, Egyptian activists and protesters played a key role in Egypt's Arab Spring. But in the end, Mubarak's presidency did not end because of what the Egyptians wanted, but because those in Washington who favoured his departure outweighed those who supported him. In other words, if the pro-Mubarak camp in Washington had prevailed, nothing that happened in Tahrir Square would have mattered. Mubarak would have remained president. America First.

Shortly after Mubarak's resignation, most of the Western media left Tahrir Square. Western governments also ended their running commentary on the political events in Egypt. Their objectives in Egypt had been achieved, and they had business next door to attend to. Egypt was old news.

On 17 February 2011, less than one week after the military took over, several people were shot as Cairo police forcefully removed protesters. The reaction from Washington and other Western capitals was muted. By the first week of March 2011, activists were growing frustrated with what they perceived as a slow pace of the transition towards civilian rule. Many believed that despite its promises of a quick transition to civilian rule, the SCAF could decide to stay in power, and all their struggles would have been in vain. They returned to the square to voice their frustration. The authorities moved in, tore up protesters' tents, and beat the protesters. Some were arrested and later tried in military tribunals.

The suspicions of the activists were soon proven right, as the military remained in power past its self-imposed six-month deadline. To be fair, the military council might have simply underestimated the amount of time necessary to achieve the goals that it had set for itself. It did not hesitate to hand over power once those tasks were completed.

But the SCAF was brutal, nonetheless. In October 2011, Coptic Christians gathered in Cairo to protest that the persecutions they suffered under the previous regime were continuing under the current one. The authorities moved in to disperse the protesters, and twenty-six people were killed in the clashes. Few people in the world who followed the events leading up to Mubarak's resignation on Western media ever heard of this incident; that shows just how unimportant human rights issues in Egypt had become to Western governments once their regime change objectives were achieved.

Some of the attention returned when the military council eventually scheduled parliamentary elections for 28 November 2011 and the Muslim Brotherhood emerged as early front-runners. Coverage of the elections indicated that the West was neither impressed with nor prepared for the prospect of an Islamist group coming to power in Egypt. Just seven months earlier, a very angry Hosni Mubarak had stressed to those in the White House who sought his removal from office the importance of an orderly transition ahead the elections, but the US government had gone ahead and forced him out.

The Islamist groups built on their early lead and eventually achieved a landslide victory in the parliamentary elections, dominating the new assembly.

Having successfully delivered the legislative elections, the military council turned its attention to the presidential elections and the new constitution. It scheduled presidential elections for 23 May 2012 and began the process of forming the Constituent Assembly, the body that would write the final constitution.

Thirteen candidates participated in the first round of presidential elections on 23 May 2012, which resulted in two front runners: Mohammed Morsi, candidate of the Muslin Brotherhood Party, and Ahmed Shafiq, candidate for the NDP and last prime minister under Mubarak. But the dominance of the Muslim Brotherhood was such that Morsi was almost assured of victory. The run-off election between the two front-runners on 15 June 2012 would be a mere formality.

The military council had invited all registered political groups to participate in talks to form the constituent assembly. On 8 June

2012, after months of argument, the composition of the Constituent Assembly was finally agreed on.

The day before the election run-off, the military council hurriedly passed new laws to limit the powers of the president and strengthen the position of the military. According to the new laws, the power to enact new laws and control the budget would lie with the military council and not the president. The ad hoc nature of the changes suggested that the SCAF was nervous about the prospects of a Muslim Brotherhood presidency or that it was perhaps acting on the advice of nervous Western nations.

In any case, the decrees never took effect. On 15 June 2012, Morsi became the first democratically president of Egypt. Shortly after taking the oath of office, he ordered senior military leaders to retire, reversed the decree of the SCAF, and set about consolidating his power.

The legacy of the SCAF will be that they were ruthless and intolerant towards demonstrations but appear to have worked hard to create a foundation for a transition to civilian rule. It left behind an elected parliament, elected president, and a broad-based Constituent Assembly. It could have written the new constitution but decided to leave it to the new civilian structures that it had created and instead focused on making the changes that directly related to elections, making them more transparent, introducing term limits for presidents, and restricting the use of emergency laws. Lastly and importantly, it handed power over peacefully to the newly elected civilian president.

Shortly after taking over, Morsi's administration convened the Constituent Assembly to start writing the new constitution.

Five months into his presidency, Morsi faced his first major foreign policy test. On 12 November 2012, the Israeli government targeted and killed a leader of Hamas in response to weeks of rocket fire from Gaza. Hamas retaliated with more rocket fire, and the conflict escalated into a shooting war. After eight days of fighting,

Morsi brokered a ceasefire which ultimately resulted in an end to the battle. The Morsi initiative was hailed as a great success by the United States, Israel, and Arab nations. Mohammed Morsi, an Islamic extremist leader who only months earlier was the stuff of nightmares for Western governments, was now a key regional player and an internationally courted statesman.

So, when Morsi was ousted in June 2013 by a military coup led by his defence minister, General Al Sisi, the news came as a surprise. After all, the ceasefire of November 2012, just seven months earlier, had shown that Morsi was a potential partner for peace in the Middle East. He had leverage with Hamas, respected Israel's positions, and had the backing of regional players such as Turkish President Erdogan. So why was he overthrown? Equally important, why was his overthrow not condemned by the West?

Despite his international charm and celebrity status, Morsi's one year as president of Egypt was a very turbulent time at home. There were constant fuel shortages and severe food inflation. These conditions, which Morsi's advisers blamed on Mubarak loyalists and other political opponents, infuriated many Egyptians and built opposition to Morsi's government. The anger was aggravated by suspicions that the Brotherhood intended to use the new constitution to introduce radical Islam to Egypt. News media was dominated by intense speculation over this issue. Deep mutual suspicion also characterised the deliberations of the Constituent Assembly, and eventually, the secular and Christian factions walked out of the assembly, leaving the Islamist factions to complete the process alone.

By the time the draft constitution was unveiled on 29 November 2012, tensions were already so high that street protests immediately broke out. On 4 December 2012, ten people were reported dead when protesters marched on the presidential palace and clashed with police. Protests continued for months while a new activist group, called the Tamarod, started petitioning for the resignation of Morsi.

Western leaders did not come out in support of the fledgling democratic processes of Egypt and the newly democratically elected President. Even when Morsi was embattled, and the democratic process appeared to be in peril.

In June 2013, the Tamarod announced that it had gathered twenty-two million signatures in its petition to oust Morsi. The defence minister issued a statement that the growing "split in society" between Morsi's supporters and their opponents might compel the military "to intervene."

It is possible that, despite their public praise for Morsi in the wake of the Israel/Hamas ceasefire, the West and Israel remained suspicious of Morsi. After all, he had broken a long-standing tradition of the Egyptian government and opened the border to Gaza. This allowed Hamas to have a steady flow of supplies. It also put Hamas in a position of strength during the ceasefire negotiations with Israel, so much so, that Hamas saw themselves as winners of the eight-day conflict, even though they lost 164 militants and civilians.

According to the UK newspaper *The Guardian*, "Hamas [emerged] stronger from Gaza war after Israel Ceasefire Deal." *The Guardian* also reported that the victory had brought a stream of regional leaders from Turkey, Tunisia, Egypt, and beyond who were proud of Hamas for "standing up to Israel."

To the extent that friends of Israel were angered by the situation, they must have been relieved to see the end of Morsi's rule, even if it came through undemocratic means. One of the reasons why Hosni Mubarak, for all his negatives, was such a close ally to the United States and to Israel was because he was decidedly opposed to Hamas and would not have opened the border. It is possible that Sisi harboured a strong inclination against the Brotherhood. He is said to have declared, "There will be no Muslim Brotherhood during my reign." (www.theguardian.com, "Sisi says Muslim Brotherhood will not exist under his reign", 6 May 2014) Subsequent events proved this to be true.

On 3 July 2013, the army suspended the government, placed the president under house arrest, and took over the daily running of the country. Field Marshall Fattah Al Sisi, defence minister in Morsi's government, became president.

The West did not condemn the coup. More importantly, some Western governments did not even acknowledge there was a coup. US Secretary of State John Kerry said that in overthrowing Morsi, military leaders "did not take over" and that they were merely "restoring democracy." (www.bbc.com, "Egypt army 'restoring democracy', says John Kerry.", 1 August 2013)"

Such statements are shameful and raise serious questions about the leadership and intentions of the United States in geopolitical matters. Egyptians sacrificed their sweat and blood to elect a president for the first time in their nation's history. There is no higher expression of democracy than at the ballot boxes. How does Morsi's overthrow by a brutal military regime that went on to kill over 800 demonstrators in one day represent a restoration of democracy?

After taking power, Sisi closed the border to Gaza. Hundreds of thousands of Muslim Brotherhood members and supporters took to the streets to protest the coup. Protesters set up a tent village on Tahrir Square and vowed not to leave until democracy was restored.

In August 2013, US President Barack Obama sent US Senators Lindsay Graham and John McCain to Egypt to "bring a message of Inclusiveness". They told protesting Muslim Brotherhood militants that they needed to "get out of the streets and get in the ballot booths." This statement was another regrettable demonstration of America's shifting priorities. The militants were in the ballot booths two years earlier. The military had no right to forcefully remove the president that these people cast their votes for. Therefore, the Senators' lecture on the significance of the ballot booth should have been directed at the coup leaders.

Sisi's response to the protests was swift and ruthless. He sent troops to clear the area. The clean-up operation was a bloodbath the likes of which had not been seen in recent Egyptian history. By some accounts, the Rabaa massacre, as it came to be known, resulted in eight hundred deaths and thousands of injuries. To put this into perspective, the total number of people killed in anti-Mubarak protests between 25 January 2011 and the resignation of Mubarak on 11 February 2011 ranged from 365 (according to Mubarak officials) to 846 (according to an investigation carried out after Mubarak's resignation).

When Tamarod and other groups were staging disruptive demonstrations in the final months of the Morsi presidency, neither Senators Graham and McCain nor anyone else went to Cairo to persuade protesters to "get out of the streets and into the ballot boxes". The message is clear and worrying: when it suits its interests, the West pulls out the democracy rule book. When brandishing the democracy rule book does not fit with its strategic interests, the West would, with equal conviction, look the other way while democracy is dismantled.

Eventually, Mohammed Morsi and thirty-five of his supporters were ordered to stand trial. They were sentenced to death on 16 May 2016. The president of Turkey criticised the decision and accused the West of hypocrisy, adding, "The popularly elected president of Egypt, chosen with 52 percent of the vote, has unfortunately been sentenced to death.… Egypt is turning back into ancient Egypt."

It was clear that the military government, having orchestrated a coup in the country, was now consolidating its position by cleansing the opposition. On 28 April 2014, *The Guardian* newspaper in the UK reported that 683 Muslim Brotherhood supporters had been sentenced to death. According to the paper, the cases "form the latest instalment of a government crackdown in which at least 16,000 people have been arrested and more than 2,500 killed since the removal of the Muslim Brotherhood's Mohamed Morsi as President last July." (www.guardian.com: "Egyptian Judge to rule on death penalty for 1200 men", Patrick Kingsley, 28 April 2014) International media, which provided 24-hour coverage of the Arab Spring, remained largely silent on this new, undemocratic reality in Egypt.

Western governments put a lot of pressure on Mubarak to resign because he allegedly ordered police to disperse protesters. Immediately after that, they used a lot of diplomatic pressure to obtain United Nations authorisation to invade Libya, allegedly to protect civilians in the aftermath of a failing insurgency. But they took no actions against the regime in Cairo that was locking up and executing people in the thousands.

This very troubling lack of consistency and transparency in the policies of Western powers, and an equally troubling disparity between their official statements and their actions behind the scenes, means that they should not have the authority—moral or otherwise—to act as global police. It also demonstrates that their involvement in Egypt was driven by their own short-term interests rather than a principled commitment to universal values and to the civic rights of the Egyptian people.

An important legacy of the Egyptian Arab Spring, therefore, must be that it exposed the inconsistent policies of Western nations and provided an incontrovertible basis for the theory that those nations use human rights and democracy only as an instrument to legitimise intervention in other countries for their own selfish interests.

PHOTOGRAPHS FROM THE ARAB SPRING IN EGYPT

During the protests that took place in Egypt in January and February of 2011, Western governments accused then President of Egypt, Hosni Mubarak, of mobilizing the police against peaceful demonstrators. The images in this section show that the protests were not peaceful. They were violent, destructive, and disruptive. Protected by Western pressure on Mubarak, the protests escalated out of control with devastating consequences that changed the course of Egypt's History.

All images and image descriptions courtesy of Reuters.

DOCUMENT DATE:
30 January, 2011

Protesters take part in a demonstration at Tahrir Square in Cairo January 30, 2011. Egyptian opposition leader Mohamed ElBaradei told thousands of protesters in central Cairo on Sunday that an uprising against Hosni Mubarak's rule "cannot go back". The banner reads: "Leave, Mubarak." REUTERS/Asmaa Waguih

DOCUMENT DATE:
02 February, 2011

Pro-government supporters of Egyptian President Hosni Mubarak
(L) clash with anti-government protesters in Tahrir square in central
Cairo February 2, 2011. REUTERS/Yannis Behrakis

DOCUMENT DATE:
03 February, 2011

An opposition demonstrator throws a rock during rioting with pro-
Mubarak supporters near Tahrir Square in Cairo February 3, 2011.
REUTERS/Goran Tomasevic

DOCUMENT DATE:
28 January, 2011

A protester runs next to a police vehicle after throwing a bag of trash at it during a demonstration in Cairo January 28, 2011. REUTERS/ Goran Tomasevic

DOCUMENT DATE:
28 January, 2011

A protester stands in front of a burning barricade during a demonstration in Cairo January 28, 2011. Police and demonstrators fought running battles on the streets of Cairo on Friday in a fourth day of unprecedented protests by tens of thousands of Egyptians demanding an end to President Hosni Mubarak's three-decade rule. REUTERS/Goran Tomasevic

DOCUMENT DATE:
28 January, 2011

Smoke billows over Cairo following clashes between protesters and police January 28, 2011. REUTERS/Yannis Behrakis

DOCUMENT DATE:
28 July, 2013

A member of the Muslim Brotherhood and supporter of deposed Egyptian President Mohamed Mursi touches the blood from pro-Mursi protesters, killed during late night clashes, at the Tomb of the Unknown Soldier, near their campsite at Rabaa Adawiya Square, in Nasr city area, east of Cairo July 28, 2013. Thousands of supporters of Egypt's Muslim Brotherhood stood their ground in Cairo on Sunday, saying they would not leave the streets despite "massacres" by security forces who shot dozens of them dead. Egypt's ambulance service said 72 people were killed in Saturday's violence at a Cairo vigil by supporters of deposed President Mohamed Mursi, triggering global anxiety that the Arab world's most populous country risked plunging into the abyss. REUTERS/Amr Abdallah Dalsh

CHAPTER 7

THE ARAB SPRING: HOW IT HAPPENED IN LIBYA

Throughout the crisis in Egypt, Libya was calm. Four days after Mubarak was forced out of office, protests broke out in the eastern Libyan city of Benghazi. Cynics would question the timing. Was Mubarak's departure a precondition for events in Libya to start? Were the anti-government factions in Libya simply encouraged by the apparent success of the protests in Egypt? Or was it pure coincidence?

What we know is that protests started as a copycat to the Egyptian protests: Organisers used flyers and social media to call for a day of rage on 17 April. Like the events in Egypt, the day chosen for the day of rage was one highly charged with symbolism and with a high potential for tensions between law enforcement and protesters. It was the fifth anniversary of deadly clashes between police and demonstrators in Benghazi, which began when protesters attacked the Italian consulate in the city.

Libyan intelligence services found out about the protests planned for 17 April 2011 and arrested one of its organisers, Fethi Tarbel, questioned and released him. The arrest of Tarbel led organisers to precipitate their protests. Demonstrators clashed with police, and according to CNN, "dozens of people were killed by security forces."

Other sources, including Human Rights Watch, put the number of fatalities in the hundreds, amidst claims that the government was firing indiscriminately into crowds.

On 20 February 2011, the US government issued a statement condemning the use of force and called on the Libyan government to "allow peaceful protests."

Saif Al-Islam Ghaddafi made a televised address to the people of Libya, in which he acknowledged the wave of change going through the region and promised that the government would make significant political reforms. He apologised for the fatalities and admitted that the army had made mistakes in its handling of the situation. He went on to say that the casualties came about because of large crowds storming the army barracks. Apparently, the crowds were so large that the army was overwhelmed and resorted to the use of force. Some arrests were made, and when those arrested were questioned, authorities found that they were predominantly poor young men from Libya and sub-Saharan Africa who had been paid and offered drugs to demonstrate. He warned that the unrest in Libya was instigated by people outside Libya. He warned that due to its tribal nature, Libya was different from Tunisia and Egypt and that if the unrests escalated unchecked, the country could degenerate into tribal war and chaos, with untold suffering and hundreds of thousands of deaths.

Well, in hindsight, he was right. Those who ignored these warnings and recklessly dismantled the government of Libya must be held to account.

It is important to note that at this point, while the US government was calling on the Libyan government to refrain from confronting peaceful protests, the country was experiencing an armed insurgency. What was referred to as "peaceful protests" was an armed militia that was made up of a combination of Libyan civilians, army defectors, and foreign mercenaries. It is also important to note that by the time the US government released its statement, the city of Benghazi was fully under the control of these militia (CNN, "A timeline of the conflict in Libya," 24 August 2011).

Three days after Saif Al-Islam's televised address in which he warned that the protesters were armed, funded, and drugged, the protesters also took the town of Misrata, chased out the army, and looted arms from its military depots. Two days after the fall of Misrata, the UN Security Council imposed sanctions on Ghaddafi and his family and referred Libya's crackdown on the rebels to the International Criminal Court.

Questions need to be asked of the decisions made by the United Nations. At the time of imposing sanctions on Ghaddafi and his family, was the UN aware that armed rebels were operating in Libya? If not, why not, and if so, why was it not helping the government to deal with the situation? In any case, why was the UN punishing a sovereign nation for cracking down on armed rebels operating within its territory and destabilising its country?

The irony is that even some Western media outlets were already using the term "rebels," not "opposition" or "civilians" or "protesters" or "demonstrators."

Two days after the UN restrictions were imposed, the European Union also announced sanctions against Libya, including a freeze on Ghaddafi's assets and an arms embargo.

Consistency check: neither the UN nor the EU imposed sanctions on Egypt or its rulers during the anti-Mubarak protests or following the Rabaa massacre of August 2013 in which the Egyptian government allegedly killed 800 civilians.

In an interview with Christiane Amanpour for ABC News, Saif Al-Islam again denied that the Libyan Air Force had fired on civilians. "Show me a single attack," he said. "Show me a single bomb.... The Air Force just destroyed arms depots." According to Saif Al-Islam, the Air Force was trying to destroy munitions to avoid them falling into the hands of rebels.

I sometimes wonder what goes through the heads of journalists. Sitting there and doing that interview with Saif Al-Islam, surely Christiane Amanpour must have known about the activities of the armed insurgency in the country. Whether or not she believed every detail he said, surely, she must have seen that a broader agenda was playing out in the country.

Throughout the 1980s and 1990s, Libyan leader Muamar Ghaddafi was renowned for strong anti-Western views. He was accused of using Libya's oil wealth to sponsor terrorist groups in the Middle East. Leading the West to regard Libya as a state sponsor of terrorism. Most prominently, it was accused of bombing a Pan Am flight that crashed over Lockerbie, Scotland, in December 1988. The United States and the United Nations imposed separate sets of sanctions on Libya over its alleged involvement in that event.

In the decade leading up to its invasion, the Libyan government pursued a policy of détente with the West. In 1999, Libya finally agreed to hand over two men suspected of involvement in the bombing of the Pan Am flight. In return, the UN lifted its sanctions on Libya.

In August 2003, lawyers of the Libyan government reached an agreement with lawyers of families of the Lockerbie victims, paving the way for the payment of $2.7 billion in compensation. The next step was for Libya to send a letter to United Nations Security Council admitting responsibility. On 19 December 2003, Libya announced that it would voluntarily give up its weapons of mass destruction and end its nuclear program.

Western leaders welcomed the actions and accepted that Libya was no longer a pariah state but a member of the peace-loving international community.

In the years that followed between 2003 and 2011, European nations turned up the charm on Libya, France and Italy invited the Libyan leader Ghaddafi to lavish state visits. British Prime Minister Tony Blair visited Libya with a large business delegation. Many

Western companies won lucrative business deals in Libya, especially in oil and gas exploration and production.

So, the events that took place in Libya in the Spring of 2011 were happening in this context of a "reformed Nation".

On 5 March 2011, Libyan rebel groups announced that the regime in Tripoli was no longer in charge and that they were the legitimate representatives of the Libyan people. Five days later, French President Nicolas Sarkozy formally recognised the rebel organisation as the official government of Libya.

On 7 March, NATO commenced twenty-four-hour air surveillance of Libya. It is not clear why NATO was doing this, who authorised it, or if it was even legal. The following day, the European Union imposed further sanctions, targeting Libya's sovereign wealth fund, the Libyan Investment Authority (LIA).

It is absolutely amazing the breadth, depth and speed of different instruments of pressure that the West applied against Libya in just over two weeks, for something that was essentially a domestic issue. Similar issues in other countries are not even covered on the European news.

Why did the European Union target the LIA?

In 2008, a banking crisis broke out in Western countries as a result of unregulated and greedy banking practices. It was the worst financial crisis since the Great Depression in the United States, and many experts believed that another depression was inevitable. Europe and the United States were bankrupt. Leaders travelled around the world to seek financial assistance from the sovereign wealth funds of cash-rich countries such as China and some Middle Eastern states. These countries provided the liquidity for Western nations to halt the economic decline and start rebuilding their economies. Communist China bailed out the capitalist West.

A Tale of Two Economies

By the time Libya was invaded in March 2011, the US economy was still feeling the effects of the financial crisis. Unemployment was stuck at 9.2 percent. The Federal Reserve had injected $600 billion into the economy through government bond purchases, and the government injected another $858 billion in fiscal policy changes (Reader, Stephen, wnyc.org, "What Happened in 2010: Jobs and the Economy," 20 December 2010).

In October 2010, China's holding of US debt reached $1,041 billion, and it decided to stop buying new debt and start scaling back (. Jeffrey, Terence P., cbsnews.com, "US Treasury: China Has Decreased Its Holdings of US Debt," April 29 2011).

By contrast, an IMF mission to Libya on 4 November 2010 found the following:

- The macroeconomic environment was strong.
- The impact of the global financial crisis on Libya was limited.
- Non-hydrocarbon growth was solid. Non-hydrocarbon GDP growth was approximately 6 percent in 2009, with overall growth projected to hit 10 percent in 2010.
- Fiscal surplus was expected to rise in 2010.
- External current account surplus was currently expected to increase to about 20 percent of GDP in 2010.
- Net foreign assets of the Central Bank of Libya and LIA consequently continued to increase and were projected to reach $150 billion by the end of 2010 (the equivalent of almost 160 percent of GDP).
- Libya's economic growth and financial position were expected to strengthen over the medium term.
- Taking into consideration the authorities' intention to continue to prioritise spending, the growth in public spending was expected to remain moderate at about 7 percent a year.

- This would allow for nominal import growth of about 10 percent a year while maintaining current account surpluses of about 20 percent of GDP.
- Such large surpluses imply correspondingly large increases in foreign assets, with the LIA and CBL's portfolio projected to reach over $250 billion by 2015.

(Reference: https://www.imf.org/en/News/Articles/2015/09/28/04/52/mcs102810)

Again, why did the European Union target the LIA? In 2011, the IMF was forecasting that Libya's portfolio of foreign assets managed through the LIA and the CBL would reach a quarter of a trillion dollars by 2015. What is the current value of this asset portfolio? Where has the money gone? Who is accountable?

In the days after France hurriedly recognised the rebels, Libyan forces recaptured most of the towns that had previously fallen to the rebels. The Guardian reported that as the rebels abandoned the strategically important oil town of Ras Lanuf and fled, they warned that "Gaddafi's army will kill half a million." Obviously, they were referring to half a million rebel fighters? Why would the Libyan government target anyone else?

By 16 March 2011, Libyan troops captured Mesrati and drew close to Benghazi. Saif Al-Islam told France-based *Euronews* that the government would have full control of the situation in forty-eight hours. Rebel forces fleeing Misrata issued pleas for help and expressed their frustration at being "abandoned" by the West.

The following day, the United Nations Security Council passed Resolution 1973 after intense lobbying of the UN Security Council members by the United States and France. The resolution authorised the use of "all necessary measures" to protect civilians.

It is not clear to me whether the UN sent an independent fact-finding mission to Libya prior to passing resolution 1973. If it did not, it would mean that the resolution was based entirely on media reports and other potentially unbalanced sources.

What is clear, is that the UN did not send an independent verification mission to Libya to establish that Libya was in material breach of the resolution, or indeed the extent to which civilians continued to be at risk after resolution 1973 was passed.

The day after the resolution was passed, French fighter jets began bombing government positions outside Benghazi. The rush to start attacking the Libyan government without an independent observer mission to establish that the government was in material breach of the sanctions demonstrates that resolution 1973 was serving the objective of the intervention rather than the intervention serving the purposes of the resolution

The problem with Western Interventions that everybody knows but nobody talks about

On 17 March, Libya was in a civil war. By all accounts, the government estimated that it was two days away from ending the bloody insurgency and restoring peace and prosperity to Libya. But France, Britain, and the United States, prevented the Libyan government from restoring peace through dubious interpretation of a resolution that they had hurriedly pushed through the United Nations Security Council. Why?

Resolution 1973 authorised the "use of all possible means" to protect civilians. But at this point, the rebels were defeated and were retreating. Internally displaced people were in UNHCR camps (see image). So exactly why did the United Nations envision civilians needing protection?

And even if the UN was concerned about the Libyan government massacring the retreating rebels, why did it not simply send a small peace-keeping force.

One week before the UN resolution was passed, France had pledged support for the rebels. It had a vested interest in installing the rebels as the legitimate government in Tripoli and could not be considered neutral in the conflict. Why was it allowed the role of a neutral enforcer of a UN resolution?

The first strikes against Libyan government targets under the UN resolution were led by French jets, shortly after French special forces had stormed the presidency of Ivory Coast, removed its leader, and replaced him with the candidate favoured by the French government.

While French jets were pounding Libya, the embattled Libyan President threatened to release details of controversial financial transactions with then French President Nicolas Sarkozy.

In the spring of 2018, Sarkozy was indicted by French courts for taking money from the Libyan government some years before the invasion. It is clear that there were both national and personal interests at play, and that these were key drivers in the invasion and subsequent destruction of Libya.

When the airstrikes started, invading powers were extremely nervous about public opinion in their respective countries and sent their propaganda machineries into overdrive. On 22 March 2011, a US fighter jet crashed in Libya. US authorities were quick to state that the plane was not shot down but had experienced a technical malfunction. Two days later, the allies transferred command of the Libya operation to NATO.

On 12 April 2011, the African Union proposed a five-point plan for restoring peace to Libya. Ghaddafi accepted it, the rebels rejected it, and NATO refused to suspend its bombing campaign which, according to government sources, was killing civilians.

Why did the United Nations not support the peace plan of the African Union?

As the conflict continued, rebels advanced steadily towards Tripoli under the protection of NATO airstrikes. On 21 August 2011, they entered Tripoli and arrested Ghaddafi's two sons. Ghaddafi himself was later captured close to his hometown of Sirte. According to some sources, NATO forces had intercepted Ghaddafi's conversation while he was speaking with Bashir Al Assad via satellite phone, homed in on his travelling convoy, and bombed it. A mob later found Ghaddafi hiding in a drainage pipe, dragged him out, humiliated him, and then shot him in the head. No one has been prosecuted for Ghaddafi's murder. There has been no independent investigation into the allegations of civilian deaths caused by the rebels and by NATO bombs, nor into the allegations that Ghaddafi was murdered by a French special forces officer embedded with the rebels and carrying orders to ensure that Ghaddafi was not taken alive.

Conclusion

The invasion of Libya demonstrates why world peace is so elusive. It raises serious questions about the actions and motives of Western countries and the United Nations in the lead-up to the intervention and beyond. In Egypt, the United States used democracy and civic liberties as a justification to pressurise Mubarak out of office (before turning a blind eye on the abuse of civic liberties by subsequent governments). In Libya, it used humanitarian concerns as a justification and has since turned its back on the humanitarian crisis caused by its invasion.

Consistency: the punitive measures adopted against Libya by individual Western nations, the European Union, and the United Nations (under pressure from Western nations) were unique. They included economic sanctions, diplomatic pressure and direct armed attacks. No other country of the Arab Spring was targeted by such measures. Western governments such as France, which strongly opposed the US invasion of Iraq in 2002, now spearheaded the invasion of Libya.

Objectivity: The case against the Libyan government was based on media reports and reports from countries that wanted regime change in Libya. Prior to the Security Council vote, there was no independent fact-finding mission to establish the validity of the reports, the extent of the threat, the measure of sanction required, or the economic, social, human, and environment impact of intervention. After the Security Council vote, the Libyan government complained but promised to comply. Notwithstanding, French jets started bombing Libya immediately following the resolution. Europe, the United States, and the United Nations did not allow time for the resolution to take effect. Further, there was no independent verification to confirm that the Libyan government was in material breach (or not, as the case might be) of the regulations.

The UN resolution called for an immediate ceasefire and the protection of civilians. Instead of enforcing an immediate ceasefire, the allies took sides in the conflict, supported the rebels and kept both the fighting and the civilian casualties going until and after they had achieved their goal of regime change.

In the process, those same civilians that resolution 1973 was passed to protect were killed by the military intervention and its direct consequences, which included a complete breakdown of institutions of government, fierce tribal wars, intense terrorist activity, human trafficking, migrant trafficking, and a flourishing slave trade.

There must be an independent inquiry, presumably by the International Court of Justice and the International Criminal Court, to establish all the motives and drivers for the invasion of Libya by foreign powers. If necessary, the statutes of these institutions should be changed so that they can initiate investigations in cases of clear violation of international law, without waiting for the case to be referred by a nation state.

Accountability: The invasion of Libya ignored the lessons learnt from Iraq. Just like Iraq, there was no assessment of the environmental, infrastructural, political, economic, or human consequences of the invasion. As was the case in Iraq, the invasion left widespread destruction and greater suffering in its wake, for which no individuals, countries, or organisations have been held to account. In 2018, Nicolas Sarkozy was indicted by a French court. However, this case related to illegal payments he was said to have received from the Libyan government prior to the invasion. He has not been indicted for his role in the invasion itself. Barack Obama has called the invasion of Libya the biggest regret of his presidency. Britain's David Cameron has refused to acknowledge his role. During the 2015 general elections in Britain, Ed Miliband, leader of the British opposition at the time, was attacked by the country's political establishment for daring to suggest that the migrant crisis in North Africa was a direct result of the Libyan policy of the Conservative government.

Death of the Humanitarian justification: One good thing that comes from the destruction and suffering in Libya is that it has lifted the veil on the sad reality that humanitarian justification of military interventions by Western powers and exposed it as a lie.

Every Western military intervention in the 21st Century – Iraq, Afghanistan, Lybia, Syria – has left the countries in a humanitarian crisis that is much worse than both the actual situation before the invasion and the worst-case scenarios that were used to justify the invasion.

In arguing the case for the invasion of Libya, Europe, and the United States repeatedly said that they could not stand by and see innocent Libyans suffering. Once the objective of regime change was achieved, they turned their backs on the escalating humanitarian suffering. Europe literally closed its gates to migrants fleeing the desolation of post-Ghaddafi Libya and has been watching passively for years as they drowned in their thousands at its [Europe's] doorstep.

National and personal interests: In the absence of the humanitarian argument and in the presence of a preponderance of evidence of the existence of other interests, there has to be an independent inquiry to establish all the motives that led to the invasion of Libya by foreign powers.

PHOTOGRAPHS FROM THE LYBIAN CONFLICT

United Nations Security Council resolution 1973 authorized the use of all means to establish an immediate ceasefire in Libya and protect civilians. Almost immediately, French air force started bombing positions and assets of the Libyan army, later joined by other nations before eventually ceding command to NATO. The air strikes did not establish a ceasefire but focused on preventing the Libyan armed forces from dealing with the armed insurrection in its territory while rebel fighters were allowed to keep fighting and committing atrocities of war. It later emerged that the rebels were supported by Special forces from Britain, France, and other countries (www.theguardian.com, "Libya conflict: British and French soldiers help rebels prepare Sirte attack", Chris Stephen, 25 August 2011).

The photographs seen here show that at the time resolution 1973 was passed by the UNSC, the United Nations High Commission for Refugees (UNHCR) already had functioning refugee centres in Libya. If the Western powers were really concerned with protecting civilians, they could have deployed support and protection to the UNHCR efforts.

The aim of the invasion of Libya was never to protect civilians, but to back a group of rebels in the pre-planned overthrow of the government of Libya.

All images and image descriptions courtesy of Reuters.

DOCUMENT DATE:
04 March, 2011

A rebel fighter fires a cannon during a battle near Ras Lanuf, March 4, 2011.

Heavily armed rebels clashed with forces loyal to Muammar Gaddafi on Friday on the outskirts of the key oil terminal of Ras Lanuf as the head of Libya's rebel council vowed "victory or death". The rebels were attacking a military base on the outskirts of Ras Lanuf, a major oil port on the Mediterranean Sea, which has a refinery, pipelines and a terminal, and the army responded with artillery fire and helicopters firing machine guns. REUTERS/Goran Tomasevic

DOCUMENT DATE:
03 March, 2011

A rebel holds a rifle as he smokes a cigarette at a checkpoint in Brega, March 3, 2011. REUTERS/Goran Tomasevic

DOCUMENT DATE:
03 March, 2011

Rebels hold a young man at gunpoint, who they accuse of being a loyalist to Libyan leader Muammar Gaddafi, between the towns of Brega and Ras Lanuf, March 3, 2011. REUTERS/Goran Tomasevic

DOCUMENT DATE:
04 March, 2011

An evacuee arrives at a refugee camp after fleeing violence in Libya near the border crossing of Ras Jdir March 4, 2011. REUTERS/ Yannis Behrakis

A rebel fighter looks at burning vehicles belonging to forces loyal to Libyan leader Muammar Gaddafi after an air strike by coalition forces, along a road between Benghazi and Ajdabiyah March 20, 2011. REUTERS/Goran Tomasevic

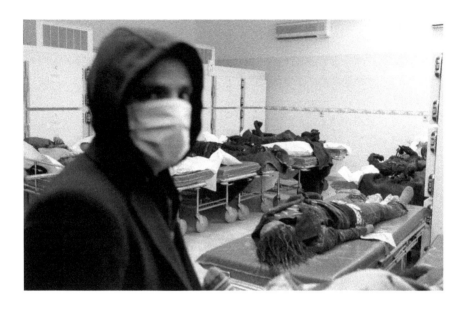

DOCUMENT DATE:
25 March, 2011

A hospital worker stands by what Libyan officials say are the bodies of civilians and soldiers killed by Western forces in Tripoli March 25, 2011. Libyan officials took journalists to a Tripoli hospital to see what they said were the charred bodies of 18 military personnel and civilians killed by Western warplanes or missiles overnight. REUTERS/Zohra Bensemra

DOCUMENT DATE:
26 March, 2011

People celebrate in a street in Ajdabiyah March 26, 2011. **Libyan rebels backed by allied air strikes** retook the strategic town of Ajdabiyah on Saturday after an all-night battle that suggests the tide is turning against Muammar Gaddafi's forces in the east. REUTERS/ Suhaib Salem

CHAPTER 8

THE ARAB SPRING: THE SYRIAN CONFLICT

There are different opinions on the causes of the Syria conflict. The generally accepted Western narrative is that the conflict started when protesters demonstrating peacefully during Syria's version of the Arab Spring were brutally attacked by the government. The narrative that has been pushed by the Syrian government and its allies is that the conflict was started by mercenary fighters acting to destabilise the country on behalf of foreign nations. Others like Britain's Prince Charles have stated that global warming was the root cause.

The truth is probably some combination of these different views. A bad draught caused a mass migration of unemployed men from rural areas to cities. As such, environmental factors could have resulted in there being a high concentration of disenfranchised people in the capital when protests broke out.

To the extent that Syria was—and remains—a proxy war of international interests, it is entirely plausible that those foreign powers that are currently fighting in Syria either directly or through their respective proxies could have played a role in initiating the conflict.

Whatever its causes, the present situation of the Syrian conflict is that many different countries are directly or indirectly engaged in military action in Syria. Some countries, such as Iran and Russia, support the government. Other countries support—in violation of international laws—one or more different rebel groups that represent their interests:

Iran has supported the Assad government since the outbreak of uprising.

In September 2015, the Russian upper house approved military intervention in Syria, and the Russian government mobilised its air force into Syria to provide support to government forces.

Saudi Arabia and Iran are the two most powerful and most influential Muslim countries in the Persian Gulf. Over the years, their rivalry for dominance in the region has fanned the flames of religious differences into a blaze of bitter enmity. Frustrated by the close ties between Syria and Iran, Saudi Arabia has made no secret of its desire for regime change in Syria. In an interview with CNN's Christiane Amanpour, the foreign minister of Saudi Arabia said that Assad had no role in the future of Syria and called on the kingdom's allies to do everything to remove Assad from power (Reference: CNN Interview of Christiane Amanpour with Saudi Crown Prince, https://saudiembassy.net/press-release/saudi-foreign-minister-al-assad-will-leave-no-doubt).

The United States, a close ally of Saudi Arabia, also stated that Assad had no role in the future of Syria. Both the United States and the United Kingdom provide logistical and tactical support to rebel groups fighting against the Syrian government, with some politicians in both countries calling for full military intervention.

Since the outbreak of the conflict, Europe and the United States have sought to weaken the Syrian government, using media propaganda, diplomatic pressure, economic and financial sanctions, support of rebel groups, and direct military action. This intervention has created an environment for terrorist groups to thrive, including ISIS.

ISIS and the illegal oil trade. Who buys ISIS oil, how, and why?

The origins of ISIS date back to 2004, when Abu Musab Al Zarqawi created a group known as Al Qaeda in Iraq. Two years later, in June 2006, Zarqawi was killed in a US strike, and Abu Ayyub al Masri replaced him as leader. Soon after taking over the leadership, al Masri created the Islamic State in Iraq (ISI). When he was killed in April 2010, Abu Bakr al Baghdadi became leader. The following year, Baghdadi sent operatives into Syria, one of whom (Abu Muhammad Julani) later became the leader of the Nusra Front terrorist group.

On 4 March 2013, the Syrian city of Raqqa fell to the opposition rebels, and Baghdadi moved to Syria, integrated elements of the Nusra Front into his organisation, and renamed it the Islamic State of Iraq and Syria (ISIS). According to the Wilson Center, "Raqqa falls to the Syrian opposition, and secular opposition groups, the Nusra Front, and ISI are all operating in Raqqa. ISI begins moving military assets to consolidate control and break into new battle fronts in Syria." (Glenn, Cameron, www.wilsoncenter.com, *"Timeline: Rise and Spread of the Islamic State"* 5 July 2016).

On 30 December 2013, rebel groups captured Fallujah and parts of Ramadi, both in Iraq. In January 2014, ISIS took over control of Raqqa from the other rebel groups and declared Raqqa the capital of the "ISIS Emirate." It continued to capture more cities and add to its territory, and on 29 June 2014, it announced the establishment of a caliphate and rebranded itself as the "Islamic State." According to CNN, the creation of the caliphate made Baghdadi "the self-declared authority over the world's estimated 1.5 billion Muslims" (CNN Library, "ISIS Fast Facts," 12 December 2017). The following day, the United States announced that it was increasing the number of its forces in Iraq.

On 3 July 2014, ISIS captured the al-Omar oilfield, Syria's largest oilfield, and a smaller gas field. Dozens of oil workers were killed in the process. The captured oilfields gave ISIS a key source of revenue. The al-Omar oilfield alone had a capacity of seventy-five thousand barrels per day but was reportedly producing about ten thousand barrels per day when it was captured. At $50 per barrel, this field alone provides revenues of $500,000 each day with a potential for up to seven times more.

The oil revenues improved ISIS's appeal and recruitment potential. Young men and women from all over the world moved to Syria to live in the new caliphate. Europeans were particularly alarmed by the number of boys, girls, and families leaving Europe to join the caliphate. In late 2014 and early 2015, four Muslim girls from East London fled to Syria via Turkey to join ISIS. In February 2015, three Muslim girls aged fifteen and sixteen travelled to Syria, apparently to become "Jihadi brides." These and many other cases sparked a strong debate in Britain. Questions were asked about why young people were abandoning their families, education, and a comfortable life to join a gang of brutal terrorists in the desert. Politicians and community leaders blamed each other, and none took responsibility. Politicians claimed that Muslim communities were radicalising children at an early age. Community leaders claimed that successive governments had neglected communities to the extent that their youths were left without hopes for the future.

But nobody was talking about the big elephant in the room: the pulling power of the oil revenues. Who was buying the oil? Why were the Western armies present in Syria and Iraq allowing ISIS to freely sell so much oil in the desert for so long.

It is difficult to know how many people travelled to Syria to join ISIS. According to some sources, approximately eight hundred people left the United Kingdom to join ISIS (Samuel Osborne, "Young British Muslims Think Isis Fighters Returning from Syria Should be Reintegrated into Society, Research Finds," The Independent Online, 17 April 2017). By early 2017, approximately half of this number had returned to Britain, and fourteen of them were sent to jail.

One month after it announced the creation of the Islamic State caliphate, IS expanded its territory into the Kurdish Yazidis. On 2 August, its fighters entered the towns of Sinjar and Zumar, and the global media lit up with alarming headlines about the persecution of Christians by IS:

The Guardian, 6 August 2014: "40,000 Iraqis stranded on mountain as Isis jihadists threaten death.... Members of minority Yazidi sect face slaughter if they go down and dehydration if they stay, while 130,000 fled to Kurdish north."

Fox News, 6 August 2014: "Militant takeover of Iraq's largest Christian city, mountaintop siege fuels calls for aid."

We already know that controversial policies of Western governments are usually preceded by heightened media activity as leaks and talking points are sent out to shape the narrative and build support. So, it was clear that something was coming.

On 11 August, Reuters reported that the United States was weighing options to rescue the people trapped on the mountain. Five days later, the US sent forces to the region.

CNN, 16 August 2014: a "heroic" mission by US and Iraqi forces has rescued the Yazidis from the mountain.

Those who thought the end of the Yazidis crisis was the end of the troops deployment do not understand the patterns of behaviour of the US government and were in for disappointment. The United States and its allies had been looking for a justification to send troops into Syria. Now they had one and were not going to walk away.

On 23 September 2014, the Pentagon announced that the United States and its partners had started airstrikes against IS targets in Syria and that it would not provide further information until the airstrikes were over. *The Washington Post* quoted Pentagon officials saying that the partner nations were Saudi Arabia, Jordan, the United Arab Emirates, and Bahrain, all of which are Saudi Arabia's regional allies. US troops remained in Syria until Donald Trump announced their withdrawal in October 2019.

The United States government knows that it is unlawful to take any kind of military action in Syria without the prior authorization of the Syrian government or the United Nations Security Council. It had tabled at least one UNSC resolution to authorize the use of military force in Syria. Well, maybe not directly. But in May 2014, the United States co-sponsored document S/2014/348, a draft resolution to refer Syria to the International Criminal Court. But Russia and China voted against the resolution. Both countries had been opposed to the Libyan resolution 1973, but eventually allowed it to pass on the understanding that the resolution would not be used to force regime change. As events unfolded in Syria, both countries were deeply distrustful of the motives of Western nations given the way they had exploited the resolution 1973 on Libya, and resolutely refused to support a UNSC resolution on Syria. Western governments and Western media promptly criticized Russia and China for refusing to support the resolution, branded them that they were insensitive to humanitarian suffering of the Syrians because they are themselves gross violators of human rights, and blamed them for the worsening situation in Syria.

'In the speeches that followed the failed vote on document S/2014/348, the representative of the United States said, "…Today is about accountability for crimes so extensive and so deadly that they have few equals in modern history. … My government applauds the vast majority of council members that voted to support and the 64 countries that joined us in sponsoring the effort to refer those atrocities to the International Criminal Court (ICC). Sadly, because of the decision of the Russian Federation to back the Syrian regime no matter what it does, the Syrian people will not see justice today. …"

The representative of the Russian Federation said, "…it is more difficult to discern the motives that led France to initiate the draft and put it to a vote, … Is it just to try once again to create a pretext for an armed intervention in the Syrian conflict?

One cannot ignore the fact that the last time the Security Council referred a case to the International Criminal Court (ICC) – the Libyan dossier, through resolution 1970 (2011) – it did not help resolve the crisis, but instead added fuel to the flames of conflict. … The deaths of civilians as result of NATO bombardments was somehow left outside its scope. Our colleagues from NATO countries refused to address the issue altogether. The even refuse to apologise, … They advocate fighting impunity but are themselves practising a policy of all-permissiveness. …"

The representative of the United Kingdom said, "…The draft resolution had the support of 13 members of the Security Council, 65 sponsors, more than 100 non-governmental organizations around the world, and the Syrian National Council. That shows the strength of international feeling on this issue. It is to Russia and China's shame that they have chosen to block efforts to achieve justice for the Syrian people. It is disgraceful that they have yet again vetoed the Security Council's efforts to take action in response to the appalling human rights violations being committed every day in Syria. …"

The representative of China said, "… China has always maintained that all parties in Syria should respect human rights and international humanitarian law. … China is firmly opposed to all violations of international humanitarian law. … [but] China believes that any action to seek recourse to the International Criminal Court (ICC) to prosecute the perpetrators of serious violations should be conducted on the basis of respect for state judicial sovereignty and the principle of complementarity. … This is our principled position. …Just now, the United States and United Kingdom and other Western countries have made totally unfounded accusations against China. That is irresponsible and hypocritical. … China has an objective and impartial position on the question of Syria. China pursues no self interest on the issue, much less shield any party, factions or persons…" (Reference: United Nations Security Council, S/PV.7180, 22 May 2014, New York)

When I started writing this book, I knew that rebel groups in Syria were acting as proxies for the United States and its allies and was really just researching evidence to demonstrate that fact to people around the world. Today, even before the book has gone to print, that sad fact is public knowledge. It makes you wonder: The United States and its allies are in Syria, illegally supporting rebel gangs, and still holding the moral high-ground against countries that are invited by the sovereign government of Syria.

There are many theories about the origin, activities, and funding of ISIS. Some people have suggested that ISIS was funded or supplied by the US military. US President Donald Trump once said that ISIS was founded by Barack Obama.

But this book is not about speculation or conspiracy theories. It is about facts, and it is a fact that in 2013, many experts estimated that ISIS was earning between US$1 million and US$3 million per day from the sale of Syrian Oil. When I heard this, as an Oil & Gas professional, I knew immediately that if those figures were true, then the US army must have known that ISIS was selling Syrian crude, and whom they were selling it to. The scale of the operation and logistics involved in exploiting giant oilfields in the desert is such that it simply cannot be conducted clandestinely. That would be the aviation equivalent of operating a commercial airport clandestinely.

In October 2014, Russian President Vladimir Putin told journalists and delegates at the 11th Annual Meeting of the Valdai club in Sochi, Russia, that "allies of the United States" were funding ISIS by purchasing oil from the oilfields it controlled, and that the United States had the power to stop the oil trade. (https://youtu.be/OQuceU3x2Ww). This information was simply ignored by the media and the international community.

In August 2016, Donald Trump, then the nominee of the Republican Party in the presidential election, said that ISIS was founded by Barack Obama. Senior Republicans weighed in to clarify that Trump implied that the president's policies created an enabling environment for the birth and growth of the terrorist group, but the presidential candidate doubled down and insisted that he meant what he said, the way that he said it. He has never retracted the statement.

What is clear is that ISIS was at the peak of its power, influence and brutality during the final two years of Obama's presidency, coincident with the deployment of US troops to Syria under the operation codenamed "Inherent Resolve" that began in August– September 2014 with the Yazidi rescue. What is also clear is that while the US Air Force was monitoring the skies and territory of Syria, ISIS was selling tens of thousands of barrels per day of crude oil. The scale of this oil and gas production operation must be emphasised. The logistics of selling enough crude oil to make just US$1 million per day as experts estimated (approximately ten thousand barrels of oil per day) involves more than one hundred tanker truck movements each day from the known refineries to the delivery point or points, assuming there is no pipeline. And if there is a pipeline, anyone can find out who is buying the oil by simply monitoring the terminal. So, in any case, following the oil trail is extremely easy.

At the peak of ISIS reign of terror between 2014 and 2016:

24 May 2014: a gunman opened fire at the Jewish Museum in Belgium. Several people were killed.

19 August 2014: ISIS published footage of what they claimed was the beheading of US journalist James Foley, who went missing in Syria in 2012.

2 September 2014: ISIS released footage of what they claimed was US journalist Steven Sotloff being beheaded.

13 September 2014: ISIS released footage showing what they claimed was the killing of British aid worker David Haines.

23 September 2014: two police officers were stabbed in Endeavour Hills, Australia. While the motives for the stabbings remained unclear, Time Magazine reported that the incident came just days after ISIS had called for random attacks on Australians and other enemies, and the 18 year-old suspect was said to have made threats against the Australian Prime Minister and waved an ISIS flag in a local mall (Ian Lloyd Neubauer, Time, *"A Teenage Terrorism Suspect Is Shot Dead in Australia After Attacking Police"*, 24 September 2014).

3 October 2014: ISIS published footage of what they claimed was the beheading of British hostage Alan Henning.

October 2014: In separate incidents, two soldiers were rammed with a car in Saint-Jean-Sur-Richelieu, Canada. One died.

October 2014: a gunman stormed into the Canadian parliament in Ottawa, and an ISIS supporter attacked two police officers in Queens, NY.

3 November 2014: 322 members of a Sunni tribe were murdered by ISIS.

December 2014: an ISIS supporter burst into a police station in Tours, France, and stabbed three police officers.

14 November 2014: The United Nations declared that Syria had committed crimes against humanity.

16 November 2014: ISIS published footage of what appeared to be the remains of American Peter Kassig, who was taken hostage.

22 January 2015: The United States claimed to have killed six thousand ISIS fighters.

24 January 2015: ISIS published footage of what appeared to be the remains of Japanese hostage Haruna Yukawa.

31 January 2015: ISIS published footage of what appeared to be the remains of another Japanese hostage, Kenji Goto.

3 February 2015: ISIS published footage of what appeared to be Jordanian pilot Moath al-Kasasbeh being burned alive while locked in a cage.

5 February 2015: American hostage Kayla Jean Mueller was reportedly killed in a Jordanian air raid on ISIS facilities in Raqqa.

10 February 2015: Mueller's family received confirmation from ISIS.

11 February 2015: President Obama requested congressional authorisation for use of force against ISIS.

15 February 2015: ISIS published footage of what it claimed were Egyptian Christians beheaded on a Libyan beach.

16 February 2015: Egypt carried out an air raid on ISIS facilities in Libya.

In terms of the legacy of the Western invasion of Libya in 2011, these incidents are a mere speck on the tip of the proverbial iceberg.

22 February 2015: ISIS published footage showing dozens of Kurdish Peshmerga fighters being paraded in cages. It is not clear what happened to them.

March 2015: ISIS reportedly killed men accused of being homosexual.

1 March 2015: ISIS released 19 of 220 Assyrian Christians it had earlier captured and imprisoned.

7 March 2015: Boko Haram pledged allegiance to ISIS.

March 2015: ISIS declared expansion of the caliphate into West Africa.

19 April 2015: ISIS published a video that appeared to show militants beheading two groups of prisoners in Libya. Ethiopia confirmed that thirty of the victims were Ethiopian citizens.

ISIS atrocities in Libya and the spread of Boko Haram are the legacy of the Western invasion of Libya. ISIS atrocities in Iraq and Syria are the legacy of the Western invasion of Iraq and its sponsorship of terrorist groups in Syria. ISIS projection of strength in Europe through daring acts of terror in European capitals would not have been possible without revenue from the sale of Syrian oil. ISIS sale of Syrian oil would not have been possible had the US army not condoned it.

16 May 2015: US special forces kill a high-ranking ISIS leader, capture his wife, and gain "significant intelligence on ISIS's structure and communications."

17 May 2015: ISIS captures Ramadi, the largest city in western Iraq.

21 May 2015: ISIS captures the ancient city of Palmyra, Syria, a UNESCO World Heritage Site with priceless monuments.

14 June 2015: ISIS conducted a suicide bombing of the headquarters of a Shia militia group in Iraq, killing more than ten people. Among the bombers was seventeen-year-old Talha Asmal. He was Britain's youngest ever suicide bomber.

19 June 2015: The US State Department, in its annual terrorism report, calls ISIS a greater threat than al Qaeda, quoting the "alarming frequency and savagery" of ISIS attacks.

24 June 2015: ISIS destroys holy sites in Palmyra.

26 June 2015: ISIS claims responsibility for a shooting at a beachfront hotel in Tunis that killed thirty-eight, mainly Western tourists, and a bomb that killed more than twenty-seven people at a mosque in Kuwait.

1 July 2015: ISIS attacked Egyptian military posts, killed seventeen Egyptian soldiers, and injured thirty others, but lost a hundred of its militants.

4 July 2015: ISIS footage shows the mass killing of twenty-five captives in Palmyra.

17 July 2015: ISIS detonates ice truck during Eid al-Fitr festivities in Khan Bani Saad. More than 120 people are killed and over 140 wounded.

August 2015: ISIS releases footage of the demolition of the two-thousand-year-old Temple of Baalshami and other antiquities in Palmyra. UNESCO calls the destruction of the temple a war crime.

In August 2015, the US Army Operation Inherent Resolve in Syria was entering its second year, and questions must be asked as to how these atrocities could take place under their noses. It was not disrupting the finance mechanism of IS or preventing its barbaric attacks. So what was it doing in Syria since August 2014?

When Russian President Vladimir Putin told reporters and world leaders in October 2014 that ISIS was selling oil to allies of the United States and that America had the power to stop the trade but had chosen not to, the international community completely ignored the revelations of the Russian president. In view of the worldwide expressions of horror and shock at the actions and evolution of ISIS, these revelations by the most powerful man in the world to a packed audience of international media, business leaders, and politicians should have been nothing less than a twenty-first-century Watergate. "ISIS-Gate." But they fell like cotton pads. Who knew what, when? Fast-forward one year later.

30 September 2015: Russia's upper house authorises military actions in Syria, and Russian jets begin striking what they called ISIS targets.

The United States immediately protested the presence of the Russians. Both the Department of Defence and the State Department repeatedly called on Russia not to send its troops into Syria. US Senator Bob Menendez said that Russia was **undermining US interests in Syria** (Richard Lardner, "US Official: Russia Risks Being Mired in Syria 'Quagmire,'" *Washington Post*, 30 September 2015).

US Interests in Syria? What were these interests, besides the extinction of ISIS?

Considering the sheer catalogue of atrocities already committed by ISIS, why would the United States, which was after all expending resources in Iraq and Syria to combat ISIS—and obviously with little or no effect—not welcome the arrival of additional resources from Russia? Was it hiding something?

November 2015: Now in the second month of its military actions in Syria, Russia repeated its allegations that American allies were trading in ISIS oil, this time specifically naming Turkey. Yet again, this bombshell statement by the President of Russia did not even make the evening news,

13 November 2015: ISIS suicide bombers kill 130 people in Paris.

16 November 2015: The United States launched its first attack against ISIS oil tankers. Finally. Would this have happened if Russia had not established a presence in Syria?

18 November 2015: US Department of Defence admits that it had been aware of ISIS oil shipments all along but decided not to hit them because it figured that the truck drivers were civilians and the US forces were eager to avoid civilian casualties. (Reference: https://www.defense.gov/Newsroom/Transcripts/Transcript/Article/630393/department-of-defense-press-briefing-by-col-warren-via-dvids-from-baghdad-iraq/)

Seriously?

Less than one week after those horrific bombings in Paris, world leaders – including the US government – were vowing vengeance against ISIS and anyone who sponsored the organization, and anyone even remotely associated with knowledge of its funding trail. At the same time, the United States government quietly admitted that it had known of ISIS single most significant source of funding and had the means to disrupt it but decided to allow it to thrive. This is without doubt the biggest foreign policy scandal of the 21st Century. And yet, it did not even make the evening news.

20 November 2015: UN Security Council calls Islamic State an "unprecedented threat to international peace and security" (SC/12132). And still, nobody – government, NGO or media – questioned the decision of US forces under "operation inherent resolve" not to destroy ISIS oil shipments and to allow the oil trade to flourish.

The fact the United States, fully aware of the threat described by the UN Secretary General, allowed ISIS to continue oil shipments and vehemently opposed Russia's decision to join the war against ISIS raises the gravest of questions about its motivations and actions in the region at the time.

24 November 2015: Turkey shoots down a Russian warplane. It was the first direct shooting incident between Russia and a member of NATO since the fall of the Berlin Wall.

Turkey claimed that it acted in self-defence because the plane had strayed into its airspace and ignored repeated calls to leave Turkish territory. Russia refuted claims that its aircraft entered Turkish airspace and produced what it claimed was evidence to support it. US President Barack Obama said that Turkey had the right to act in self-defence.

Russia renewed its claims that Turkey was purchasing ISIS oil on an industrial scale and had shot down its jet to hide evidence of the illicit trade. It called Turkey an "accomplice to terror" and warned of "serious consequences."

The downing of a Russian military aircraft by a NATO member in November 2015 was the closest the world had come to a nuclear war in decades. The significance of this incident cannot be overstated, and yet no lessons. Nations and citizens were terrified of what might come next and quietly prayed for de-escalation. The fate of billions of peace-loving people in the world depends on the interests and brinksmanship of a handful of individuals and nations that have placed themselves above international law and institutions, aided by media organisations that have vested commercial interests in covering up the murderous greed of their respective governments with a complex web of lies, spin and propaganda.

International Law in the Syria Conflict

Is the presence of Russian forces in Syria legitimate under international law?

To the extent that Russia was invited by the Syrian government, its presence in Syria is legitimate. Notwithstanding, its actions in Syria must still comply with the various international treaties on armed conflict, such as the agreements on the treatment of civilians and captive combatants and the use of conventional and nonconventional weapons.

Is the support by Western and regional nations of rebel forces in Syria legitimate under international law?

Support of armed opposition groups by an external state is a violation of international law. The 1984 ruling of the International Court of Justice in the case of *Nicaragua vs United States,* provides jurisprudence for this violation.

Is the designation of the Assad regime as illegitimate by the United States and its Allies binding under international law?
No.

Summary

The situation in Syria appears incredibly complex. But that is only because the nations with vested interests in Syria need a degree of confusion to conceal their interests and actions. So, they fabricate complexity.

The reality is very simple. There are two groups of combatant forces in Syria: those who were invited by the Syrian government and those who were not. In the absence of a UN resolution authorising the use of force in Syria, any state or nonstate actors engaged in military actions in Syria without the consent of the Syrian government are violating international law. Period. They share a responsibility for destabilising the country and causing suffering to its people.

There is the moral argument that Assad is an evil man who has murdered tens of thousands of his own people.

First of all, this has not been proven in an unbiased forum. The world has learnt that just because Western Powers and their allies shout something repeatedly does not mean that it is true. And even if that was true, international rule of law requires that it cannot be up to individual nations to execute their version of justice. This is the duty and prerogative of international institutions. If nations are frustrated with the functioning of the international system, they must invest in meaningful reforms that will make it more effective. Taking the law into their hands is not an option. No country will tolerate its citizens taking the law into their own hands whenever they feel frustrated with the national judicial system.

There must be an independent international investigation into the allegations by Russia that NATO member-states were knowingly purchasing Syrian crude oil from ISIS. This investigation should be started by the International Court of Justice and the International criminal court, without waiting for a formal request from a member-state.

Similarly, there must be an independent international investigation into the complex relationship between the United States and ISIS, including but not limited to the condonement of crude oil transports and the air-dropping of equipment by the US air force into ISIS-controlled territory, inadvertent or not.

CHAPTER 9

UKRAINE

In the winter of 2013, events began to unfold in Ukraine that would bring the world to the brink of a major war. It began with the refusal by Ukraine to sign a trade agreement with the European Union. It ended with—well, it has not really ended. Eventually, the president of Ukraine was forced to flee the country, and his replacement signed the trade agreement. Russia's attempts at damage limitation resulted in the greatest stand-off between world powers perhaps since the Cuban missile crisis.

The fact a simple disagreement between Ukrainians over the policy of their government escalated into one of the most dangerous and polarising military and economic conflicts of the twenty-first century demonstrates the urgent need for an effective model for international conflict avoidance and resolution.

The cases studied in this book show that conflicts do not simply erupt out of nowhere. There is always a background and a build-up phase, during which there are important opportunities to avoid conflict. When these opportunities are not exploited, conflict escalates.

Unfortunately, what we see is countries that not only refuse to use the obvious opportunities for de-escalation, but invest in the fabrication of a complex web of lies and deception to escalate the situation to a crescendo that justifies their ultimate objectives – at immense human and economic cost.

Following the collapse of the Soviet Union, the European Union saw an opportunity to expand its zone of economic influence by absorbing former Soviet Republics through the policy of *Osterweiterung* (eastward expansion). Russia was scrambling to maintain economic relations with and some degree of regional influence over the same states. From the turn of the century, these conflicting interests were marked by escalating rhetoric and a race to sign the different states into their respective blocs. In 2013, they finally collided in Ukraine, and each side blamed the other for the causes and consequences.

Background

On 18 November 2011, the presidents of Russia, Belarus, and Kazakhstan signed a treaty to commence work towards the creation of a Eurasian Economic Union (EEU) by 2015. Russian President Vladimir Putin expressed a desire to eventually extend the union to include all former Soviet Republics, except Latvia, Estonia and Lithuania, which had already joined the European Union in 2004 as part of the largest enlargement to date.

Russia has always expressed strong concerns about an eastward expansion of the European Union which, in its opinion, was harmful to its own existing economic and trade ties with the former Soviet States.

Moldova, Ukraine, and Georgia were invited to join the Eurasian Economic Union. But the European Union also invited the same countries to join its bloc.

In August 2013, Ukraine applied to attend the EEU as an observer. At about the same time, it was engaged in talks with the European Union towards a Deep Comprehensive Trade Agreement (DCTA), which EU officials hoped would be signed at a summit in Lithuania on 29 November 2013.

A few weeks before the summit, Ukraine informed the EU that it would not sign the DCTA because the Ukrainian Parliament had rejected key EU conditions and expressed concern over potential conflicts with existing treaties between Ukraine and Russia. Ukraine instead proposed a tripartite trade agreement involving Ukraine, Russia, and the EU that would consider existing trade relationships. Russia agreed to participate in the proposed tripartite talks. The EU did not. Instead, it continued to press Ukraine to sign the DCTA.

It is not clear why the EU rejected the proposal of tripartite talks with Russia and Ukraine. After all, Russia's concerns about the impact of the DCTA on its businesses and investments in Ukraine were both understandable and legitimate.

On 21 November 2013, Ukraine's President Viktor Yanukovych formerly pulled out of the EU trade deal, and with that, he crossed the Rubicon.

Following the announcement on 21 November that the EU deal was off, several hundred protesters went into the streets to object to the decision. The crowds increased as opposition leaders, including Yulia Tymoshenko, called for more protests to put pressure on the government to reverse its decision. Police used conventional methods, including tear gas, to disperse crowds. On 29 November 2013, Ukraine attended the EU Summit in Vilnius but did not sign the DCTA. At this point, the protesters changed their demands and started calling for the outright resignation of President Yanukovych.

Protests were also becoming increasingly violent and disruptive. On 1 December 2013, demonstrators transformed Maidan Square in Kiev into a tent city and clashed frequently with the police. Several days later, they vandalised and toppled a statue of Lenin.

Western leaders came out in full support of the protesters, urging them not to back down and to show their leaders that the destiny of their country was their hands. The president of the European Parliament maintained a running commentary on Twitter. From 4

December 2013, senior European officials started visiting the protest square.

On 10 December 2013, US Assistant Secretary of State for European and Eurasian Affairs Victoria Nuland visited Maidan Square to show solidarity with anti-government protesters. She was accompanied by the US ambassador to Ukraine.

This was extraordinary. Senior politicians from Europe and the United States, standing shoulder-to-shoulder with disruptive protesters in another country, in blatant violation of international agreements on non-interference in the internal affairs of another nation.

Quite apart from the legal aspects, the reverse scenario would be simply unthinkable: Russian parliamentarians flying to Greece to support violent anti-EU demonstrators; Russian cabinet ministers travelling to New York City to join in disruptive anti-government demonstrations; Chinese cabinet ministers travelling to Mexico and Cuba to stage huge anti-US protests. There would be an immediate outcry in the West about such "aggressive" and "reckless" actions. Once again, the media, whose duty it is to provide fair and balanced coverage, failed to call out the double standards and violations of international law regarding Ukraine's sovereignty. Instead, they aligned their coverage and narratives firmly with Western governments' support for the protesters.

It is important to note at this point that the 2010 election in Ukraine gave President Yanukovych a clear democratic mandate for his pro-Russian agenda. That is what he stood for, and it is what the people of Ukraine chose at the polls. It should also be noted that the Ukrainian Parliament's concerns about the preconditions of the EU trade agreement were totally justified. None of these issues were addressed by rioting gangs in the streets.

On 6 December, the embattled Ukrainian president travelled to Sochi to meet with his Russian counterpart to discuss their "strategic partnership." To some in the West, this was proof that Russia had influenced the Ukraine government to walk away from the DCTA.

One week after his meeting with Putin and with the situation in the streets of Ukraine deteriorating, Yanukovych met with opposition leaders in an attempt to defuse the tensions. But they did not reach any agreements. Two days later, the EU announced a formal suspension with talks with Ukraine on the DCTA.

On 17 December, Yanukovych went back to meet President Putin, who pledged to buy $15 billion of Ukraine debt and also reduce the price of gas sold by Gazprom to Ukraine by one-third. The Russian assistance was bitterly criticised by the street activists, but one week later, amid growing protests, Ukraine received the first disbursement of $3 billion.

Demonstrations were suspended over Christmas and New Year's but resumed in the second week of 2014, with both sides even more entrenched in their respective positions. President Yanukovych responded to the resumption of protests by passing new laws that banned protests in the centre of Kiev, but protesters simply defied the ban and violently resisted attempts by the police to remove them. On 22 January 2014, three people were killed in clashes between demonstrators and police. The European Union increased pressure on the government of Ukraine, and President Yanukovych held a new round of talks with the opposition, which again failed to reach an agreement. The US government also threatened to impose sanctions on Ukraine if violence continued in the streets.

That week, Yanukovych's prime minister announced his resignation, and the president went on a four-day sick leave. Such was the pressure on the Ukrainian government.

The opposition refused all concessions from President Yanukovych, including key ministerial positions, and demanded fresh elections. In a show of good faith, Yanukovych reversed the anti-protest laws, but the move backfired terribly. Protests grew in number and became more violent. Demonstrators attempted to storm the Kiev Cultural Centre the day after the annulment.

On 6 February 2014, Reuters reported, "A senior Kremlin aide accused the United States on Thursday of arming Ukrainian 'rebels' and, urging the Kiev government to put down what it called an attempted coup, warned it could intervene to maintain the security of its ex-Soviet neighbour."

The revelation that the government of the United States was potentially arming protesters in another country was extraordinary to say the least. Yet, it was largely ignored by the mainstream media. This incident showed that mass media was influencing international conflict situations in a major way by suppressing important news stories and projecting disinforming narratives, while conflict-avoidance mechanisms of international institutions were weak and ineffective. The world was at the mercy of Western governments and Western mass media, and they showed no mercy.

The following day, Reuters again reported, "A conversation between a State Department official and the U.S. ambassador to Ukraine that was posted on YouTube revealed an embarrassing exchange on U.S. strategy for a political transition in [Ukraine]." It said, "The audio clip, which was posted on Tuesday but gained wide circulation on Thursday, appears to show the official, Assistant Secretary of State Victoria Nuland, weighing in on the make-up of the next Ukrainian government."

But it was more than a weighing-in. It was *the* game plan.

The United States of America was actively plotting regime change in Ukraine. To this end, it either planned the disruptive riots in the country or hijacked them.

A transcript of the conversation courtesy of the BBC, with comments by correspondent Jonathan Marcus, can be found on the network's website.

On 14 February 2014, Russia again issued a warning that the European Union was seeking a "sphere of influence" in Ukraine.

On 17 February, it purchased a further $2 billion of Ukraine debt, which drew an angry reaction from demonstrators, again resulting in fatal clashes with police.

The US government imposed a travel ban on twenty members of the Ukraine government, whom they said they considered responsible for violent confrontations between forces of law and order and protesters. But President Yanukovych continued to underscore that his government was against violence and called the opposition to a truce. Vitaly Klitchko said the president had given him assurance that the protesters' camps would not be removed. Foreign ministers from Germany, France, and Poland announced that they were travelling to Kiev to attempt to resolve the conflict. Their visit would end in Yanukovych's abdication.

In the early hours of 20 February, ahead of the arrival of the EU foreign ministers, a bizarre and bloody series of events took place in Kiev and marked a turning point for Ukraine. These events culminated in what became known as the Maidan massacre.

To Western governments, these events were the incontrovertible evidence that the government of President Yanukovych was brutal and undemocratic. To Russia, it was further proof that the unrest in Kiev was masterminded and armed by foreign powers.

A BBC investigation identified an opposition protester, who confirmed that during a tense but peaceful stand-off between police and protesters in the morning of 20 February, he took position in the Kiev Conservatory and fired shots at the police lines using a rifle that had been given to him the previous day. At the time, the Kiev Conservatory building was controlled by protesters. The shots he fired forced the police to retreat. The protesters advanced on the retreating police lines, until they were forced to open fire.

The BBC report states that the protester sniper's story is corroborated at least partially by Andriy Schevchenko, then an opposition member of parliament and part of the Maidan movement, who it says received a series of calls from the leader of the riot police at the square.

""He calls me and says, 'Andriy, somebody is shooting at my guys.' And he said that the shooting was from the Conservatory."

As events unfolded, the calls from the police officer apparently became more panicked.

"I kept getting calls from the police officer, who said: 'I have three people wounded, I have five people wounded, I have one person dead.' And at some point, he says, 'I am pulling out.' And he says, 'Andriy I do not know what will be next.' But I clearly felt that something really bad was about to happen."

Reference: Gatehouse, Gabriel, bbc.co.uk, *"The Untold Story of the Maidan Massacre,"* 15 February 2015.

https://www.bbc.com/news/magazine-31359021?print=true

In all, more than 50 people died in the Maidan massacre and up to 130 people by some accounts.

On 21 February 2014, government and opposition leaders signed a six-point plan brokered by the visiting European foreign ministers. The full text of the agreement is available on the internet.

The day after the agreement was signed, parliament voted to remove Yanukovych from power. Yulia Tymoshenko was released from Jail, and Yanukovych fled to Russia. Two days later, he was indicted in Ukraine over the deaths of protesters.

According to *National Geographic*, there are fifteen million native Russians in Ukraine, concentrated in the eastern and southern regions. Of all the former Soviet Republics, Ukraine has the highest percentage of native Russians. Russia has close cultural and economic ties with these regions, and over the years, it has invested heavily in industry in the eastern regions, which are considered the economic powerhouse of Ukraine. Russia also has a defence interest in Ukraine. The two countries share a long common border and Russia's Black Sea fleet is based in Sebastopol, Crimea. An anti-Russian government in Ukraine could constitute a serious threat to the national security of Russia especially in times of tensions between Russia and the West.

For all these reasons, Russia's concerns about what goes on politically in Ukraine are understandable and in line what other countries do to maintain the economic and political stability of their allies and ensure their own economic interests and national security. And yet, for years, Russia has been patiently appealing for dialogue between itself and Europe to establish a framework of mutual respect of interests. But Europe has rejected and ridiculed the calls.

Reacting to the overthrow of Yanukovych, Russian Foreign Minister Sergei Lavrov called his US counterpart John Kerry and accused the opposition of breaking the EU-brokered agreement and staging a coup. He urged Mr. Kerry to use the leverage of the United States over the Ukrainian opposition to bring the renegade opposition back to the full and complete implementation of the terms of the agreement. The United States government did not do that.

The Russian president called German Chancellor Angela Merkel and expressed his grave concern over the unilateral actions of the opposition and urged the European Union to take urgent actions to bring the opposition back into compliance with the peace plan.

Nothing happened.

Following the inaction from Washington, Berlin and Brussels, Moscow then issued a statement saying that its government would not deal with the leaders of an armed mutiny in Kiev. The Russian parliament approved a bill authorising the president to take all necessary measures to "protect Russian interests." Some reports claimed that the Russian government ordered 150,000 troops to its border with Ukraine.

In the eastern regions of Ukraine, where the population is predominantly Russian-speaking, protests broke out against the new leadership in Kiev and quickly developed into an armed opposition.

From 27 February into the first week of March, a series of events took place in Crimea which fundamentally changed the relationship of the West with Russia. Armed men seized the airport and parliament and set a date less than two months away for a referendum on whether Crimea should remain part of the Ukraine or join Russia.

These developments—clearly unforeseen by Europe and the United States—must have dimmed Ukraine's lustre as a Western target. Western business would have been eagerly waiting to set up in Ukraine and exploit the industrial areas in the eastern part of the country. But an armed conflict would make this goal impossible (or difficult, at best).

Western leaders struggled to find a response to the new turn of events. Their view was that these protest movements were instigated (or at least supported) by Russia. Therefore, on 6 March 2014, EU leaders met in an emergency summit to "find ways to pressure Russia to back down and accept mediation" (Reuters). But the Russians repeatedly denied that they had influenced the events. European leaders sent a group of military observers from the Organisation for Economic Co-operation and Development to Crimea, but they were denied entry.

On 7 March, President Obama joined the desperate attempts to prevent the break-up of Ukraine. He called President Putin, but after an hour-long conversation, the Russians said that both sides were no closer to resolving the issue.

The Crimean Referendum took place on 16 March 2014, as planned. More than 97 percent of the people voted to join Russia. On 18 March, President Putin signed a treaty to annex Crimea into the Russian Federation. NATO condemned the action and said the Russian government had embarked on a "dangerous path." (Reference: Siddique, Haroon, and Yuhas, Alan, www.theguardian. com, *Putin Signs Treaty to Annex Crimea as Ukraine Authorises Use of Force,*" 18 March 2014).

Unable to control events on the ground, and unwilling to concede defeat, Europe and the United States started declaring sanctions against Russia to respond to what they called extremely aggressive behaviour and blatant violations of international law. They also questioned Russia's references to its "sphere of influence" and claimed that Russia has no right to Ukraine.

Europe's condemnation of the United States over the Iran JCPOA was a matter of principle. Not a principled defence of international agreements, but the principle that there is a special bond between Europe and the United States. This bond enabled them to create a Bismarckian world order that benefitted both. And now the United States was breaking the special bond and going it alone.

The prevailing opinion in the West is that Russia is aggressive and invaded Ukrainian territory for no good reason. But when you analyse the events that happened in the lead-up to Russian involvement in Ukraine, it is hard not to see the hand of the United States and the European Union in shaping events.

The conflicts analysed in this book (Egypt, Libya, Syria, Ukraine) have the acronym ELSU. Each of them highlights a different element of Western geo-policy. The Ukraine conflict brought the Bismarckian elements to the fore: you violate international law; cause immense destruction, death, and suffering; and get your constituents to believe—despite the preponderance of glaring and incontrovertible evidence to the contrary—that it was all your opponent's fault.

How?

On 7 February 2014, the United States was telling the angry Ukrainian demonstrators in the streets of Kiev that their violent and disruptive protests to force concessions from their democratically elected leaders were a civic right. On 7 March 2014, the United States was telling Ukrainians in the streets of Donbas that their violent and disruptive protests to demand the restoration of their democratically elected leader amounted to acts of terror.

On 10 December 2013, the United States declared that it had a "moral obligation" to support the brave Ukrainian protesters in the streets of Kiev and dispatched Victoria Nuland, its assistant secretary of state for European and Eurasian affairs, to Kiev to do just that.

The evidence available in the public domain shows that she even went beyond just supporting the protesters. She actively conspired to decide who should rule Ukraine. On 7 March 2017, the United States declared than any support by Russia for the Ukrainian protesters in the streets of Donbas was an act of aggression and would be met with the strictest sanctions. Unilateral sanctions. Extraterritorial sanctions. And Europe fully supported them.

The United States unconditionally supports and provides military protection to Israel and Saudi Arabia, invaded Iraq to liberate Kuwait, regularly infuriates China with its commitment to Taiwan's security, and causes tensions against North Korea with its unconditional support for Japan and South Korea. It facilitated or condoned the overthrow of the democratically elected Muslim Brotherhood in Egypt—perceived to be hostile to US interests—and is either actively destabilising Venezuela or undermining the efforts of the government to stabilise the country. The United States will defend its interests anywhere in the world by any means necessary. To many Europeans, Americans, and their allies, this policy is entirely justified.

But curiously, the same Europeans, Americans, and their allies maintain that Russia has no right to complain about the systematic dismantling of its strategic interests in Eastern Europe by Europe and the United States. In fact, Europeans now widely believe EU claims that Russia is an aggressive country. Curious, given the following:

In 1990, the United States invaded Iraq. In 2001, it invaded Afghanistan and started a war that is still going on. The following year, it again invaded Iraq and removed its president. It has since stationed missile systems in Eastern Europe, forced the Egyptian president out of office, facilitated or condoned a coup that removed his successor from office, invaded Libya, sponsored terror groups in Syria with the declared objective of removing its president, tested China by sending warships into waters declared out of bounds by China, pushed North Korea to the brink of war by carrying out military drills just outside its territorial waters, and crippled numerous countries with harsh and arbitrary sanctions.

And yet, it is "gravely concerned" by the aggressive policies of Russia which, between 1999 and the onset of the Ukraine conflict, has not started any conflict outside the former Soviet territory.

Thanks to the relentless anti-Russian propaganda by Western governments and media, citizens of Europe and the United States view Russia as an aggressive country that threatens world peace.

Summary

Politics in post-Soviet Ukraine has been defined by the choice of regional integration: Europe or Russia?

Following the 2004 presidential election, the pro-Russian candidate Viktor Yanukovych declared victory. His opponent alleged widespread fraud and, with the support of Western countries, launched disruptive protests that became known as the Orange Revolution. The West forced the president to cancel the elections and rerun them in a manner favourable to the pro-European candidate, Viktor Yushchenko. Yushchenko won the rerun and, with it, claimed a mandate to integrate Ukraine into the European Union.

Yushchenko did not deliver the improvements he promised would come through increased cooperation with Europe. On the contrary, the economy deteriorated so badly that even the EU cooled off its Ukraine aspirations. By the time his five-year tenure was over, his chances for re-election were minimal.

During the 2010 elections, Yanukovych came back from the opposition benches and won a resounding victory. Even the European Union conceded that his election was clear and fair.

As with the 2004 election, the 2010 election was a referendum on the geopolitical orientation of the country, and therefore, Yanukovych's victory was a mandate to reintroduce pro-Russian policies and strive for greater integration with Russia.

As mentioned earlier, in 2013, Yanukovych informed the European Union that the Deep Comprehensive Trade Agreement would conflict with existing agreements with Russia and proposed a tripartite meeting to find the best solution for Ukraine, Russia, and Europe. Russia agreed. The EU did not.

When protests broke out in Kiev, senior officials from the European Union and the United States both encouraged and participated in the protests. This is against the principle of non-interference in internal affairs of sovereign nations.

The protesters were armed, violent, and destructive.

Apart from participating in the protests, Western countries used a combination of media propaganda, financial constraints, and diplomatic pressure to severely hamper the ability of the Ukraine government to manage the protests. In addition, there is evidence that US government officials were directly involved in plotting the course of a new government in Ukraine.

At a critical moment of events, foreign ministers of Poland, Germany, and France travelled to Kiev to broker a roadmap to peace. That day, police were ordered to leave the scene of protests. As they were retreating, unidentified snipers fired both at demonstrators and at police. Both the police and the demonstrators returned fire. The incident resulted in dozens of fatalities.

The meeting with the foreign politicians went ahead, and a peace plan was agreed upon and signed by the government and the opposition. Under the provisions of the plan, the president would stay in office, and the opposition would gain important concessions.

The following day, the opposition breached the agreement and held a vote in parliament to remove the president from power and replace him with an interim president. Yanukovych fled to Russia, and the Russian government declared that an armed coup had been orchestrated in Kiev.

Pro-Russian constituencies who won the 2004 elections, lost the rerun, spent five years in democratic opposition, and won the 2010 election fair and square had reason to feel aggrieved. They started their own round of protests, calling for greater autonomy or total cessation of their regions.

Europe and America, who had encouraged protesters in Kiev to get up and march, criticised the protesters in Donbas as terrorists.

Those who had openly supported the Kiev protesters branded Russia a state-aggressor and introduced a slate of unilateral sanctions against Russia.

There needs to be an independent investigation, presumably by the ICJ and the ICC, into whether support of disruptive protests by the European Union leadership and the US government constitutes a breach of international law.

The independent investigation should extend to the events that took place in the Maidan square in the early hours of 20 February 2014 and establish if there were hidden snipers acting to escalate the peaceful stand-off between the police and the protesters, whether or not there was an involvement of actors outside Ukraine, and who they were.

As events were unfolding in Ukraine in 2014, it was clear to me that European Union and United States were acting not in the interest of Ukraine's democracy, but in their own interest – taking advantage of national grievances to muscle Russia out of the attractive Ukraine market and establish trade ties of their own. When I started writing this book, one of the objectives was to lay out the evidence for this.

As the book is undergoing its final edit, Donald Trump, the President of the United States has taken this further. He suggested that Joe Biden, who was Vice President of the United States during Ukraine uprising and effectively in charge of Ukraine policy, might have used his position to pursue personal financial interests in Ukraine. These are serious accusations. President Trump has not provided any evidence Former Vice President Biden has denied in the strongest terms any wrongdoing in Ukraine. So far, this is being treated as an internal political issue in the United States and typically will end there. That is wrong. The Ukraine conflict has caused extreme suffering to families in Ukraine, Russia and beyond, so these allegations must go beyond the internal politics of the United States and strengthen the case for an international investigation.

Europe and the United States broke international law and destabilised Ukraine for their own interests. Both national interest and, if the allegations above are proven, personal interests. Just as was the case in Libya.

PHOTOGRAPHS FROM THE UKRAINE CONFLICT

In 2010, Ukrainians elected Viktor Yanukovych as President, with a mandate of greater integration with Russia, after a disastrous five-year mandate of pro-European president Viktor Yushchenko. In the Fall of 2011, the government of Yanukovych and the Ukrainian Parliament refused to sign a Deep Comprehensive Trade Agreement with the European Union because a) it would jeopardise existing agreements, and b) the Ukrainian Parliament had failed to ratify certain terms demanded by the European Union.

Pro-European activists in the Ukrainian capital Kiev launched street demonstrations in protest of the President's decision. The protesters soon got the backing of political leaders in the European Union and the United States.

The photographs here show protests that were violent, destructive and disruptive. Incredibly, they also show United States officials, on the ground, encouraging the protests and meeting with opposition forces, ostensibly to plot the overthrow of the government.

All images and image descriptions courtesy of Reuters.

DOCUMENT DATE:
19 January, 2014

Pro-European integration protesters attack a police van during a rally near government administration buildings in Kiev January 19, 2014. Up to 100,000 Ukrainians massed in the capital Kiev on Sunday in defiance of sweeping new laws aimed at stamping out anti-government protests. The rally, the biggest this year in a cycle of pro-Europe protests convulsing the former Soviet republic for the past two months, was spurred by the legislation rushed through parliament last week and which the opposition says will lead to a police state. REUTERS/Gleb Garanich

DOCUMENT DATE:
20 January, 2014

A pro-European integration protester sits in a burnt police bus after a rally near government administration buildings in Kiev January 20, 2014. Protesters clashed with riot police in the Ukrainian capital on Sunday after tough anti-protest legislation, which the political opposition says paves the way for a police state, was rushed through parliament last week. REUTERS/Valentyn Ogirenko

DOCUMENT DATE:
20 January, 2014

A pro-European integration protester aims his pneumatic gun towards riot police during clashes in Kiev January 20, 2014. Protesters clashed with riot police in the Ukrainian capital after tough anti-protest legislation, which the political opposition says paves the way for a police state, was rushed through parliament last week. REUTERS/ Vasily Fedosenko

DOCUMENT DATE:
23 January, 2014

A pro–European integration protester fires off fireworks towards riot police during clashes in Kiev January 23, 2014. Ukrainian opposition leaders emerged from crisis talks with President Viktor Yanukovich on Wednesday saying he had failed to give concrete answers to their demands, and told their supporters on the streets to prepare for a police offensive. REUTERS/Valentyn Ogirenko

DOCUMENT DATE:
22 January, 2014

A pro-European protester throws a burning tyre during clashes with riot policemen in Kiev January 22, 2014. The European Union threatened on Wednesday to take action against Ukraine over its handling of anti-government protests after three people died during violent clashes in Kiev. REUTERS/Gleb Garanich

DOCUMENT DATE:
20 January, 2014

Ukrainian riot police officers react after being hit by a petrol bomb during clashes with pro-European integration protesters in Kiev January 19, 2014. Protesters clashed with riot police in the Ukrainian capital on Sunday after tough anti-protest legislation, which the political opposition says paves the way for a police state, was rushed through parliament last week. REUTERS/Stringer

DOCUMENT DATE:
19 February, 2014

Interior Ministry members stand in formation during clashes with anti-government protesters at Independence Square in central Kiev February 19, 2014. Ukrainian President Viktor Yanukovich warned his opponents on Wednesday that he could deploy force against them after what he called their attempt to "seize power" by means of "arson and murder". REUTERS/Olga Yakimovich

DOCUMENT DATE:
10 December, 2013

U.S. Assistant Secretary of State for European and Eurasian Affairs Victoria Nuland walks in the opposition camp at Independence square in Kiev, December 10, 2013. U.S. Secretary of State John Kerry urged the Ukrainian government on Tuesday to "listen to the voices of its people" after President Viktor Yanukovich's decision to spurn a pact with the European Union sparked mass protests. REUTERS/Andrew Kravchenko/Pool

DOCUMENT DATE:
11 December, 2013

U.S. Assistant Secretary of State for European and Eurasian Affairs Victoria Nuland (C) distributes bread to protesters next to U.S. Ambassador Geoffrey Pyatt (L) at Independence square in Kiev December 11, 2013. Scores of Ukrainian riot police withdrew on Wednesday morning from a protest camp after moving against protesters overnight in the authorities' biggest attempt yet to disburse weeks of protests against President Viktor Yanukovich. REUTERS/ Andrew Kravchenko/Pool

DOCUMENT DATE:
07 February, 2014

Ukrainian opposition leaders Oleh Tyahnybok (L), Vitaly Klitschko (2nd R, back) and Arseny Yatsenyuk (R) pose for a picture with U.S. Assistant Secretary of State for European and Eurasian Affairs Victoria Nuland during a meeting in Kiev February 6, 2014. An east-west struggle over Ukraine turned nastier as Moscow accused the United States of fomenting a coup and Washington pointed a finger at Russia for leaking a recording of U.S. diplomats discussing how to shape a new government in Kiev. U.S. officials did not challenge the authenticity of what seemed to be a phone call bugged about 12 days ago and which also contained an obscene comment by Assistant Secretary of State Victoria Nuland about the European Union's efforts to work with Washington in support of the Ukrainian opposition. Picture taken February 6, 2014. REUTERS/Andrew Kravchenko/Pool

HOW THE UNITED STATES DEALS
WITH PROTESTS AT HOME

All images and image descriptions courtesy of Reuters.

DOCUMENT DATE:
10 July, 2016

A demonstrator protesting the shooting death of Alton Sterling is detained by law enforcement near the headquarters of the Baton Rouge Police Department in Baton Rouge, Louisiana, U.S. July 9, 2016. REUTERS/Jonathan Bachman TPX IMAGES OF THE DA

CHAPTER 10

ECONOMIC WARFARE

Having been on top of events in Kiev, the EU and its allies suddenly found themselves on the back foot as events escalated in the Ukrainian regions of Crimea and Donbas.

Between 3 March and 31 December 2014, the EU issued eighteen different sets of punitive economic measures against Russian companies, individuals, institutions, and the government. In the same period, the United States issued four executive orders and two pieces of legislation.

Throughout 2015 and 2016, sanctions were maintained, and new sanctions were introduced.

Russia retaliated with economic sanctions against the West. Among these sanctions: certain individuals from the EU, America, and Canada were banned from entering Russia; Ukrainian airlines were banned from transiting through Russia; and importation of meat and dairy products, fish, vegetables, fruits, and nuts originating from countries that imposed economic sanctions against Russia were halted.

It is important to note that sanctions were not merely a symbolic measure of condemnation. It was war. One element of a multipronged attack that also included attempts of global isolation and sabotage, and whose stated objective was to cripple the entire Russian economy and force Moscow to reverse its actions in Crimea. The West was at war with Russia. Western leaders spoke openly about their economic warfare that targeted the total destruction of Russia's economy. On 1 September 2014, *The Telegraph* published an article captioned "Cameron: We Will Permanently Damage Russia's Economy." According to the article, Prime Minister David Cameron vowed to "turn up the ratchet" on Vladimir Putin and warned that "Western sanctions [against Russia] would permanently damage the Russian economy." The article stated, "Moscow banks are running short of funding as investors pull capital out [of] the country, while the rouble and the Russian stock market are falling."

In April 2014, President Obama was touring Southeast Asian nations to promote his "pivot to Asia" and used the opportunity to lobby countries to join his economic coalition against Russia.

As the rouble continued to fall, many in Russia believed that investors acting on behalf of Western governments were deliberately attacking the currency:

On 2 September 2015, *Sputnik* quoted the Mexican newspaper *El Universal* as saying that there was an agreement between the United States and Saudi Arabia to drop global oil prices as part of a financial war America was waging against Russia. It said that while economic growth in the United States was affected by the global economic recession of 2008, Russia had rapidly grown to become the world's most important energy supplier. Together with Beijing and three other nations, Moscow had created the BRICS Bank, which was playing an increasingly important role in international transactions and seen to be a rival to Bretton Woods institutions and the hegemony of the US Dollar. Since Russia received most of its revenue from oil and gas, the United States sought to weaken Russia by conducting a "dumping strike" against the entire oil and gas industry.

Three days later, Mikhail Fradkov, head of Russia's Foreign Intelligence Service, told Bloomberg that the United States and its allies were seeking regime change in Russia by attacking the rouble and manipulating world oil prices.

These are serious allegations that go beyond the United States and Russia. The drop in global commodity prices had a serious negative impact on global economic growth.

Most people would appreciate how difficult it is to transform a low-income country into a medium-income country in just a couple of decades, and lift millions of people out of poverty in the process. The idea that a developed country can launch calculated attacks to damage the fragile growth of another country is unacceptable in modern civilized society.

On 4 December 2014, Vladimir Putin said in his annual presidential address to the Federal Assembly in the Kremlin's St. George's Hall that the Russian government knew exactly who was profiting from speculation against the Russian rouble and had "the tools to punish them."

At the time of this speech, in December 2014, Russia was hurting. The United States was two years from its next presidential election and feeling untouchable. But President Putin's speech seemed to suggest that Russia was planning its revenge.

The following month, President Obama gave his annual state of the union address before the joint houses of Congress, in which he said the Russian economy was "in tatters." This was his celebration of, in his view, the success of the various policies that had been targeted at harming Russia. In effect, he was declaring victory in the economic war.

Russia was hurting. The United States was bragging. And there was not even an independent evaluation of the accusations used to justify such large-scale damage to a country's economy. These accusations were, in my assessment, mainly unjustified.

An enemy of progress:

By mid-2018, Chinese company Huawei was already a global Telecom giant. In July 2018, its year-to-date shipments of mobile handsets passed the 100 million mark. Just two weeks later, it passed Apple as the world's second largest maker of handsets, On 25 December 2018, Huawei announced that it had sold 200 million handsets in 2018, These were not low-quality products. When Huawei released its P30 series of mobile handsets in April 2019, these were generally hailed by industry experts as the best handset in the market at the time. Most importantly, most serious industry analyses revealed that Huawei was several years ahead of Western companies in the development and roll-out of 5G telephony technology.

Negative sentiment against Huawei began building in the United States. The company's Chief Financial Officer was arrested in Canada on 1 December 2018 and held in Canada pending extradition to the United States. 10 days later, the President of the United States said that he would intervene for the release of the Executive, also daughter of the founder of Huawei, if China agreed to the terms of his trade deal. Sounds like a kidnapping and ransom.

In February 2019, the United States government started pressuring governments in Europe and around the world to exclude Huawei from 5G network development contracts.

On 19 February 2019, Ren Zhengfei, the Founder and CEO of Huawei said "The US cannot crush us", and added a day later that the arrest of his daughter was a politically motivated act to erode Huawei's technological lead in the 5G space.

As interest among European countries in Huawei's 5G technology remained strong, US Secretary of State said on 21 February that countries using Huawei technology shall be viewed as a risk to the United States.

In May 2019, the US government banned Huawei from the United States, and banned the company from including US technology such as Google apps in its handsets sold in other countries.

In the spring of 2020, when it was clear that Huawei was still growing robustly as a telecom provider, the US government issued a global ban on any company in any country that uses US technology from supplying Huawei.

The Telecom industry is one of the most heavily regulated industries in the world. Regulations protect patents, consumer rights, privacy, and security. If a company is suspected or accused of violating regulations, the competent regulators review the alleged violations and issue a comprehensive report of breaches. They fine the company and outline a catalogue of changes that the company is expected to make within a defined timeframe.

This is not what happened in Huawei's case. To date, no formal charges have been filed against Huawei for specific regulatory or statutory violations. Therefore, it appears the company's only violation is that it is a Chinese entity. The Huawei case shall be seen by future generations as a country using its power to bully an innovative company out of markets at the expense of consumers and general human progress.

In 2018 – 2019, a European Consortium called Nord Stream 2 AG built a pipeline to deliver Russian natural gas to Western Europe. Nord Stream 2 is a consortium that consists of five independent European energy giants: Gazprom (Russia), Uniper (Germany), Wintershall (Germany), Royal Dutch Shell (Netherlands / UK), and Engie (France). By the end of 2019, the pipeline construction was about 90% complete when the US government imposed sanctions on the project intended to hinder its completion altogether.

On 21 December 2019, BBC wrote that "The Trump administration fears the pipeline will tighten Russia's grip over Europe's energy supply and reduce its own share of the lucrative European market for American liquefied natural gas." (www.bbc.

co.uk, "Nord Stream 2: Trump approves sanctions on Russia gas pipeline", 21 December 2019).

On 16 February 2020, World Oil Magazine wrote, "Asked about Russian efforts to circumvent U.S. sanctions on the pipeline by completing it on its own, U.S. Energy Secretary Dan Brouillette said 'they can't' -- and dismissed claims that project owner Gazprom PJSC will face only a short delay.

'It's going to be a very long delay, because Russia doesn't have the technology,' Brouillette said in an interview at the Munich Security Conference on Saturday. 'If they develop it, we'll see what they do. But I don't think it's as easy as saying, well, we're almost there, we're just going to finish it.' " (www.worldoil.com, "*U.S. says sanctions mean Russia can't finish Nord Stream 2 pipeline*", Patrick Donahue and Matthew Miller, 2 February 2020)

Enemies of progress!

The Belt and Road initiative is an infrastructure network spanning four continents and 76 countries according to Forbes (www.forbes.com, "As China's 'Belt And Road' Initiative Replaces U.S. On Global Stage, The Implications For Energy And Trade", Ken Silverstein, 5 December 2019), which noted that "The great paradox now in geo-political circles is that the United States is becoming more isolationist while China is increasing its global presence, … China is thus accelerating its international trade ties while gaining more access to new technologies."

The United States started criticising the initiative and privately pressing allies not to take part in it. On 20 December 2019, it created its own U.S. International Development Finance Corporation. It would be sad to think that the IDFC was not created out of a genuine concern to provide solutions for the suffering of countries around the world, but just to blunt the appeal of the Chinese Belt and Road Initiative. On 16 June 2020, the Engineering & Technology Magazine reported that the US Ambassador to Brazil had told Brazilian media that the United States would help fund the country's 5G network via the USIDFC on condition that Huawei was excluded (eandt.theiet. org, "US offers to fund Brazil's 5G, if Huawei is excluded", E&T editorial staff, 16 June 2020).

CHAPTER 11

MEDIA AND DIGITAL WARFARE

In the winter of 2013–2014, Europe and the United States saw an opportunity to extend their economic influence in Ukraine. They attempted to achieve this using a method that worked in Egypt and Libya in 2011, and Ukraine nine years earlier: disruptive street protests. This time, things did not go according to plan. Russia made a last stand to salvage its own interests in Ukraine, and the country disintegrated into civil war, just like Libya

From that moment on, senior politicians in Europe and the United States identified Vladimir Putin's Russia as the greatest threat to US and European interests around the world. In a sense, this was true. The Rubicon had been crossed, and Russia would never again stand idly by and watch the US and Europe shift the rules, break-and-take.

But Western leaders could not sell that narrative to their citizens. They had to create a more sinister narrative to justify their hostile stance towards Russia. And thus, began a coordinated campaign to undermine Russia—economically, diplomatically, as well as through media and cyber-attacks. Everything that transpired in Russo-American and Russo-European relations from 2014 to date must be seen in this light.

In January 2017, the outgoing US government accused Russia of "meddling in the internal affairs of the United States." It was referring to allegations that Russian entities had hacked into the computer systems of the Democratic Party and released sensitive information with the intention of influencing the outcome of the electoral process in favour of Republican Party candidate Donald Trump and against the party of incumbent President Barack Obama, who had led the international multipronged campaign to crumble Russia.

Even if Russia interfered in the 2016 US presidential election, it cannot be seen in isolation, but must be seen in the context of two years of unrelenting Western pressure on Russia, and near-constant US intervention in other countries' affairs, including Russia's. Russia had repeatedly complained about attempts by Western governments (including and especially the United States) to interfere in Russian politics and destabilise the nation. In 2015, the Russian parliament passed a law prohibiting non-governmental organisations (NGOs) that were engaging in "undesirable" activities. The list of NGOs targeted was expanded in 2016 and again in 2017.

Russia firmly believes—and there is evidence to support that— that Europe and the United States conspired and facilitated a coup in Ukraine that overthrew a pro-Russian president, installed a pro-Western one, and severely damaged Russia's strategic interests.

From mid-2014 through 2015, the West automatically accused Russia of everything. On 17 July 2014, a Malaysian Airlines flight from the Netherlands to Kuala Lumpur crashed into a field in the Ukraine. British Prime Minister David Cameron said that ten British citizens had perished in the crash and warned that those responsible would pay. Later, he said it was "increasingly likely that MH-17 was shot down by a separatist missile" fired from an area controlled by pro-Russian rebels. No evidence for the allegations was provided.

The day after the incident, President Obama held a press conference in which he accused pro-Russian separatists in Ukraine of bringing down the plane using surface-to-air missiles supplied by Russia. Three days later, Obama said that Vladimir Putin had direct personal responsibility for the actions of the separatist rebels. No evidence was provided. In May 2016, a US lawyer working for an Australian law firm named Vladimir Putin personally responsible for the downing of the MH-17.

Aviation accidents are among the most tragic and sobering occurrences in modern life. If a country or organisation is accused of either carrying out or aiding the deliberate downing of a commercial airliner, it can have devastating consequences for its international image, its prosperity, and indeed its security. Maybe this is the reason why, whenever there is an aviation incident, governments typically call on all stakeholders to abstain from speculation, share everything they know with the dedicated team of investigators, and wait for the outcome of the independent investigation. But in the case of MH-17, the governments of the United States and the United Kingdom came out within twenty-four hours of the incident and pointed accusing fingers at Russia. This kind of behaviour is reckless and irresponsible. To see the greatest Western democracies rushing to conclusions and pouring more fuel to explosive situations, while Russia, supposedly the brutal aggressor, showed restraint and calmness, was disconcerting, to say the least. Russia's ambassador to the United Nations, Vitaly Churkin, accused the United States and its allies of "trying to prejudge the outcome [of an investigation] with broad statements and insinuations."

Russia denied any knowledge of, or association with the tragic incident and claimed that pro-Russian fighters in eastern Ukraine could not be held responsible for the shooting of the airliner, either. According to Russia, whatever the causes of the incident, the ultimate responsibility lay with the government of Ukraine for failing to close the airspace over the conflict zone to commercial traffic. Control of the commercial airspace and safety was the responsibility of the government of Ukraine, as it is standard international practice to divert commercial air traffic away from active war zones.

It is worth mentioning that finding Russia responsible for the downing of the MH-17 on the basis or argument that the suspected missile system was made in Russia for the Russian armed forces, is both convenient and incomprehensibly childish, because the missile systems are readily available for any state or non-state actor to acquire.

Sadly, even basic conclusions like this were left unchallenged by mainstream media.

Just as in the Maidan shootings, it is worth asking who stood to gain from the shooting of MH-17.

By the summer of 2014, Ukraine was risking territorial break-up. Russia had already annexed Crimea and was under the first wave of Western sanctions. Though ambitious, Russia was careful not to bite more than it could chew in Ukraine. At the same time, the separatists in the Ukraine had made significant gains and pushed government forces out of the region. The last thing both Russia and the Donbas separatists needed was to attract additional pressure to themselves by shooting down a Malaysian aircraft full of Dutch citizens.

On the other hand, associating the Donbas rebels with the shooting of a commercial airliner with European nationals would further discredit the rebels and potentially attract sympathy and even support for the efforts of the government in Kiev.

Unfortunately, the truth about the shooting of the MH-17 lies buried somewhere in the lies, accusations, and counteraccusations of powerful and overly ambitious nations.

PART III

A NEW AND HUMANE WORLD ORDER

CHAPTER 12

GOVERNMENTS AND MEDIA: A TOXIC ALLIANCE

In all the cases considered in the ELSU study, Western media played a key role, and it was not an objective one.

In Egypt, the media was instrumental in putting pressure on Mubarak to resign but did not act in equal measure to shine the light on the coup against the Morsi government and the subsequent brutal cleansing of the Brotherhood.

In Libya, the media was instrumental in making the case for invasion by repeatedly portraying the armed insurgency as a movement of peaceful demonstrations. So much so, that the UN resolution 1973 was passed in urgency not least by the increasingly urgent and desperate media reports. It was also instrumental in concealing both the violations of resolution 1973 by the allies and the scale of human rights abuses by the rebels during the conflict. Once the objective of regime change was achieved, the media left Libya. The country, once the most prosperous in Africa under Ghaddafi, is now a failed state with two rival governments, a raging civil war, rampant tribal wars, thriving terrorist activity, human trafficking, the first sustained market for human slaves since more than 200 years, and a primary route for smuggling migrants to Europe in treacherous crossings of the Mediterranean that have claimed more than 10,000 lives and continue to do so. The media has made sure that this chaos in Post–Ghaddafi Libya effectively goes unreported. A free and objective media would have stayed in Libya, highlighting the contrast between pre- and post-invasion Libya, shining a light on the ongoing consequences of the invasion, making parallels with Iraq and holding the invading powers to account until they invest time and resources to stabilize the country.

In Syria, the media is doing governments a great favour by using the narrative of Assad as a brutal monster to conceal the fact Western governments are acting as state sponsors of terrorism in the country. In particular, the media effectively ensured that the scandal of the US Army tolerating ISIS oil trade never entered the living rooms of Western households. Latest after the shock and horror caused by the terrorist bombings in Paris, a free and objective Media should have, and would have turned the spotlight and the pressure on the US government for tolerating ISIS oil trade that enabled them [ISIS] to raise the funds to finance such audacious acts of terror in the heart of Europe.

Despite constitutional guarantees for freedom of expression, most countries have a group-think culture that discourages divergent opinion and penalises critics of controversial government policies. In other words, when it comes to criticizing their governments for highly controversial, high-stakes policies, citizens of so-called Free World are as scared of the ruthlessness of their governments as in any other country, regardless of their social or political status. On 24 April 2015, Ed Miliband, then leader of the opposition, defined the crisis of migrants dying in the Mediterranean in attempts to cross from North Africa to Europe as a direct consequence of the invasion of Libya, and blamed David Cameron's government for its part in the invasion. The comments drew sharp criticism from the prime minister and his associates, calling the comments "ill-judged" and "opportunistic." Conservatives sought to portray Miliband as unpatriotic and said he had implied that the British prime minister was a "murderer." Miliband was forced to backtrack and explain himself: "If you listen to my words, if you listen to the speech I gave, it is clear what I'm saying, which is about the failure of the international community, and the British government, and David Cameron, to engage in that post-conflict planning which should have been done." He then went on to say that his party "supported military action to avoid the slaughter Gaddafi threatened in Benghazi."

When the British government accused Russia of poisoning Sergey Skripal in March 2018, Jeremy Corbyn, then leader of the opposition, expressed the view that the government should not rush to conclusions before all the evidence had been assembled and considered. This drew a barrage of criticism from the government and the media, many of whom accused Corbyn of being Putin's puppet. One newspaper showed Corbyn on its cover dressed as a communist worker. The media was attempting to bully the leader of the parliamentary opposition into submission. Unlike Miliband, Corbyn remained resolute, much to the frustration of the British political establishment. Instead, he doubled down on his warnings: "This horrific event demands first of all the most thorough and painstaking criminal investigation, conducted by our police and security services.... To rush way ahead of the evidence being gathered by the police, in a fevered parliamentary atmosphere, serves neither justice nor our national security."

But even Corbyn had to show that he was on Team UK: "Labour is of course no supporter of the Putin regime, its conservative authoritarianism, abuse of human rights or political and economic corruption," before going on to offer the strongest endorsement by a senior Western politician of the ideas in this book: "However, that does not mean we should resign ourselves to a 'new cold war' of escalating arms spending, proxy conflicts across the globe and a McCarthyite intolerance of dissent."

The question of political legitimacy is an age-old one, and Western governments, it seems, have found a useful partner in legitimising their attacks on sovereign countries: the media.

"The obverse of the legitimacy of power is the power of legitimacy" (Inis Claude).

CHAPTER 13

A NEW GLOBAL AGENDA

When most people talk about a new world order, they are referring simply to a change of "pecking order" under the same archaic rules – one country is the top dog and gets to impose its will on other nations.

To most, the idea of equality and impartial rule of law among nations is utopic and not worth striving for. Pretty poor, for a race that, in its infinite arrogance and narcissism, has declared itself the most civilized race to ever inhabit the earth.

I do not care about the specifics of the world order that emerges after the coronavirus pandemic, just as long as it is anchored in the principles of universal human rights and sovereignty of nations. In the third decade of this twenty-first century, any new world order that is not based on the rule of international law, maintained by independent international institutions, and applied equally to all nations regardless of race, colour, size or power shall be archaic, inadequate, dangerous and unacceptable. Just as national institutions safeguard equality of citizens before a Nation's laws, so too must international institutions safeguard equality and rule of law among Nations.

As the first quarter of the 21st Century nears its end, it is vitally important that all people and all governments should commit to the defining Agenda of our time: to finally make humanity an advanced civilization which truly values every human life, and truly respects the principles of equality and justice among all people.

Surely, there will be many detractors claiming that some countries have attained the status of Advanced civilization and that their citizens enjoy equality before the law.

There is a whole different book to be written about why this may not necessarily be the case. But even if it was, most countries that boast democratic foundations at home, act as bullies in the international community. They treat the citizens of other countries as dispensable collateral in the pursuit of their selfish national and personal greed.

At the level of nations, we humans are still just a bunch of barbarians tricking, deceiving, invading, destroying each other.

Consider the earth as a metaphorical country, GLOBUS, with the present-day nation states as its citizens. So, the United States, Russia, Libya, Syria, Cameroon are all individual citizens of GLOBUS. Would you say that GLOBUS has the rule of law, equality before the law and justice for all? Or would you say it has the justice of, by and for the rich and powerful?

So long as the rule of law among nations is not guaranteed, internal freedom and security are f leeting as they can be ended in the twinkle of an eye by the desperate acts of peoples that have been frustrated in their native lands by the destructive interventions of advanced 'democratic' governments. Even in the most peaceful of countries, when you talk to people in the streets, there is an underlying anxiety that is related to this sad truth.

What should be done?

Equality before the law means that only competent institutions have the right to hold a nation-state guilty and shall do so after due consideration of all evidence and prove it beyond all reasonable doubt. Further, all member states of the United Nations have signed up to the principle of peaceful resolution of disputes.

I. Legal Framework:

For there to be true and lasting peace and prosperity in the world, there must be international rule of law. For there to be international rule of law, there must be a legal framework. This already exists and is summarized in Part I.

II. Organs of conflict resolution:

Institutions of global rule of law already exist. The UN, the UNSC, the ICJ, the ICC. Countries just need to respect them, and Citizens can achieve a lot by demanding that their governments stop undermining these institutions, comply with their statutes like every other nation, and work to strengthen them where necessary.

Unfortunately, the world has instead chosen to abdicate its powers for conflict management to the United States. Nowadays, it is perfectly acceptable for the United States to accuse a country, investigate the country, declare the country guilty, never present a shred of evidence supporting the condemnation (and if any evidence is presented, it usually turns out to be incorrect), sentence the country to a sanctions regime (of which the United States decides the type, severity and duration), and enforce the sanctions – all by itself. This is like a country where the most powerful clan or clans make and enforce the law, as was the case in England before the Magna Carta.

Many have pointed out that the United States is reluctantly thrust into the position of global Sheriff due the weakness and ineffectiveness of global institutions. I respectfully disagree, and maintain that the situation is quite the opposite, International institutions are weak and without credibility because they are frequently used and abused by Western Powers for their own purposes. When institutions refuse to be manipulated, they are systematically bullied and undermined.

In the Spring of 2020, the United States accused China of gross endangerment of the world in the wake of the novel coronavirus. The 'charges' were presented in daily news briefings by US officials, and varied from involuntary exposure through gross incompetence, to calculated germ warfare. The punishment decided by the US was the threat of further trade tariffs, economic and financial sanctions. China published a detailed chronology of its handling of the pandemic, and of its collaboration with the WHO and international experts, including US experts and the US government. The US provided no proofs for its accusations. Notwithstanding, it was actively recruiting countries to join in its attacks against China and its plot to isolate and weaken the country in much the same way that it sought to isolate and weaken Russia in 2014 - 2017. This type of behaviour is bullying that, ironically, is no longer tolerated anywhere in modern society – not even in elementary schools.

At the same time, the United States launched fierce and vicious attacks against the WHO, accusing the Organisation of collusion with China to endanger the world with the coronavirus. Without providing any proof, it declared and implemented punishment against the Organisation: total withdrawal of its funding (in the midst of a pandemic).

Weeks later, it [the United States] attacked the International Criminal Court for daring to investigate alleged human rights abuses by US Servicemen in Afghanistan and promptly imposed sanctions against the investigating judges. But the US routinely refers other countries to the ICC when it suits its purposes (Libya, Syria).

Is this really the kind of world you want your children to grow up in? The sad truth is that for millions of people, it is. Like in a community that is under Mafia control, there are two sets of people: those who are oppressed by the system and are powerless to do anything about it, and those who benefit from the system and do not want to do anything about it.

III. <u>Economic Sanctions:</u>

The combined impact of US sanctions and other measures against different countries costs the global economy trillions of dollars every year. The adverse effects of these sanctions on citizens of those countries are similar to the effects of an armed attack.

Only international institutions shall have the right to impose economic and financial sanctions on a country and shall do so based on proof beyond reasonable doubt after careful consideration of all available information from all parties.

The declaration of economic and financial sanctions by one country against another country shall be seen as an act of aggression and treated as such by the relevant international institutions.

IV. <u>Code of diplomatic conduct</u>

All countries shall adhere to a code of diplomatic conduct, which shall include a zero-tolerance towards bullying. A credit system shall be maintained by international institutions for code offenders, similar to global carbon credits systems. Fines shall be used to strengthen global institutions.

V. <u>Code of Media conduct</u>

The media industry has long declared itself an independent check against the abuse of political power. An international code of media conduct would strengthen this objective.

A global regulation shall be applied to all media outlets classified as national or transnational, with particular reference to those involved in the reporting on international conflicts. The objective is not to stifle the freedom of operation of media, but to guard against ethics violations and symbiosis between media and powerful national governments.

VI. Commitment to post-intervention reconstruction

The United Nations Security Council shall not approve an international intervention, unless the resolution includes a financial commitment to carry out an economic, social, and environmental impact assessment (ESEIA) prior to the intervention, and to ensure that all adverse impacts are removed, and the country left in a net positive state. ESEIAs are nothing new. Sovereign countries routinely demand this exact same condition from corporations that intend to carry out economic activities within its national territory. There is no reason why the same standards should not be applied to sovereign states that propose "well-intended" interventions in other countries, as a guarantee of their good intentions.

In this context, the United Nations Security Council shall pass a resolution requiring all nations that have led international interventions in the 21st Century to return to those countries, stabilize and reconstruct at their own cost, and leave in a net positive situation.

VII. Final Remarks

If we really want to leave a better world for future generations, we need to do a lot more than worry about the environment. We need to care about the way we treat each other, as individuals and as nations. Environmental damage can cause hardship and suffering, gradually over decades or centuries. Conflicts between Nations can end the human race as we know it, today.

REFERENCES

1. http://www.express.co.uk/news/uk/572179/Boris-Johnson-Special-Forces-SAS-Libya-migrant-crisis
2. https://www.globalcitizen.org/en/content/the-refugee-crisis-explained-in-3-questions/
3. http://indianexpress.com/photos/picture-gallery-others/european-union-migrant-crisis-over-700-feared-dead-in-multiple-mediterranean-shipwrecks-2825298/
4. http://www.express.co.uk/news/uk/586548/Mediterranean-migrant-crisis-British-spies-hunt-African-people-smugglers
5. http://www.telegraph.co.uk/news/worldnews/islamic-state/11459675/Greeces-defence-minister-threatens-to-send-migrants-including-jihadists-to-Western-Europe.html
6. http://www.reuters.com/article/us-iraq-war-anniversary-idUSBRE92D0PG20130314
7. http://www.itv.com/news/2015-04-20/timeline-of-europes-intensifying-migrant-crisis/
8. https://www.theguardian.com/world/2015/jun/22/migrants-hungary-border-fence-wall-serbia
9. http://www.aljazeera.com/news/middleeast/2011/01/201112515334871490.html
10. http://www.aljazeera.com/news/middleeast/2011/01/201112617427113878.html
11. *Financial Times*, "Clinton and Obama: An American Rift over

an Egyptian Despot," 27 October 2016.

12. bbc.co.uk, "Egypt Parties End Deadlock over Constitutional Panel," 8 June 2012.

13. www.nytimes.com, "Kerry Says Egypt's Military Was 'Restoring Democracy' in Ousting Morsi," 1 August 2013.

14. www.theatlantic.com, "What Kerry Should Have Said in Egypt," 6 November 2013.

15. www.usatoday.com, "Hamas Marks Anniversary of 2012 Israel Conflict," 13 November 2013.

    *https://www.aljazeera.com/news/2019/08/massacre-calls-justice-remain-years-190814141159728.html

16. www.theguardian.co.uk, 22 November 2013.

17. www.theguardian.co.uk, "Egyptian Judge Sentences 720 Men to Death," 28 April 2014.

18. CNN, "2011 Libya Civil War Fast Facts," 4 April 2016.

19. www.bbc.co.uk, "Libya Protests: Ghaddafi's Son Warns of Civil War," 21 February 2011.

20. www.abc.net.au, "The Full Story ... Ghaddafi's Son Admits Mistakes by the Army," 21 February 2011.

21. www.bbc.co.uk, "Libya Protests: Ghaddafi's Son Warns of Civil War," 21 February 2011.

22. Curto, Stefano, siteresources.worldbank.org, "Sovereign Wealth Funds in the Next Decade."

23. Reader, Stephen, wnyc.org, "What Happened in 2010: Jobs and the Economy," 20 December 2010.

24. Jeffrey, Terence P., cbsnews.com, "US Treasury: China Has Decreased Its Holdings of US Debt," April 29 2011.

25. www.theguardian.co.uk, "Gaddafi's Army Will Kill Half a Million," 12 March 2011.

26. Aljazeera.com, "Libyan Rebels Reject African Union Roadmap," 12 April 2012.

27. Taylor, Alan, *The Atlantic*, "Libya's Escalating Conflict," 9 March 2011.

28. The Atlantic, "Three Months of Civil War in Libya," 25 May 2011.

29. The Atlantic, "The Battle for Libya's Oil: On the Frontlines of a Forgotten War.

30. http://www.reuters.com/article/us-libya-events-idUSTRE77 K2QH20110822: "Timeline: Libya's Uprising against Muammar Gaddafi," 22 August 2011.

31. https://en.wikipedia.org/wiki/Ukraine%E2%80%93European _Union_Association_Agreement

32. Reuters.com, "Putin Aide Warns U.S. on Ukraine, Says Russia Could Act," 6 February 2016.

33. Reuters.com, "Leaked Audio Reveals Embarrassing U.S. Exchange on Ukraine, EU," 6 February 2016.

34. bbc.co.uk, "Ukraine Crisis: Transcript of Leaked Nuland–Pyatt Call," 7 February 2014.

35. Gatehouse, Gabriel, bbc.co.uk, "The Untold Story of the Maidan Massacre," 15 February 2015.

36. Siddique, Haroon, and Yuhas, Alan, www.theguardian.com, "Putin Signs Treaty to Annex Crimea as Ukraine Authorises Use of Force," 18 March 2014.

37. Strauss, Julius, *The Telegraph*, "Moscow Accuses EU of Meddling in Ukraine," 27 November 2004.

38. BBC, "On This Day, 27th December. 2004: Yushchenko Wins Ukraine Election Re-Run."

39. BBC, "Profile of Viktor Yushchenko."

40. http://www.consilium.europa.eu/en/policies/sanctions/ ukraine-crisis/history-ukraine-crisis/

41. https://www.state.gov/e/eb/tfs/spi/ukrainerussia/

42. *Moscow Times*, "Obama Says Western Sanctions Have Left Russian Economy 'in Tatters,'" 21 January 2015.

43. BloombergView, "No Obama, Russia's Economy Isn't 'in Tatters.'"

44. Glenn, Cameron, www.wilsoncenter.com, "Timeline: Rise and

Spread of the Islamic State," 5 July 2016.

45. CNN: Interview of Christiane Amanpour with Saudi Crown Prince.

46. Ryan, Missy, and Mason, Jeff, Reuters.com, "U.S. Weighs Options to Evacuate Desperate Yazidis from Iraqi Mountain."

47. voanews.com, "Pentagon: US Evacuation of Yazidis from Iraqi Mountain Unlikely," 13 August 2014

48. dw.com, "US Rescue Operation for Yazidis on Iraq's Mount Sinjar 'Less Likely,'" 14 August 2014

49. pbs.com, "Yellow Journalism."

50. Holmes, Oliver, and Borger, Julian, *The Guardian*, "Nuclear Deal: Netanyahu Accuses Iran of Cheating on Agreement," 30 April 2018.

51. Channel 4, "McMafia Author Misha Glenny on Sergei Skripal Case: 'It Looks More Like State than Crime,'" 6 March 2018.

52. BBC, "Russian Spy: Boris Johnson Warns Kremlin over Salisbury Incident," 6 March 2018.

53. Dodd, Vikram, Harding, Luke, and MacAskill, Ewen, *The Guardian*: "Sergei Skripal: Former Russian Spy Poisoned with Nerve Agent, Say Police," 7 March 2018.

54. *The Guardian*, "Guardian View on the Russian Spy Attack: Sergei Skripal and the Sowing of Discord: Editorial," 9 March 2018.

55. Wiltshire Police Federation, "Salisbury Poisoning: Gloves Failed to Shield Sergeant from Novichok."

Lightning Source UK Ltd.
Milton Keynes UK
UKHW011130070920
369492UK00001B/67